RED, WHITE & BLUE STAR QUILTS

16 STRIKING PATRIOTIC & 2-COLOR PATTERNS

JUDY MARTIN

CROSLEY-GRIFFITH PUBLISHING COMPANY, INC.

GRINNELL, IOWA

Crosley-Griffith Publishing Company, Inc. is an imprint of C & T Publishing, Inc., P.O. Box 1456, Lafayette, CA 94549.
Publisher: Amy Barrett-Daffin
Acquisitions Editor: Roxane Cerda
Creative Director: Gailen Runge
Book design and typesetting: Judy Martin
Illustrations: Judy Martin
Proofreading and editing: Judy Martin and Steve Bennett
Photography for Starlight Medallion: Lauren Herberg of C & T Publishing, Inc.
Photography for America, the Beautiful and page 11: Brian Birlauf, Birlauf & Steen Photography, Denver, CO
Photography for pages 3 and 14: Judy Martin and Steve Bennett.
Photography for all remaining quilts: Terry Doran of Mittera Creative & Technical, Des Moines, IA
Photography assistants for all remaining quilts: Judy Martin, Steve Bennett, and Todd Hanson
America, the Beautiful is an original design by Will Bennett.
All other quilts are original designs by Judy Martin.

Library of Congress Control Number: 2021945646

Printed in the USA

10 9 8 7 6 5 4 3 2

Attention teachers: C & T Publishing encourages the use of our books as texts for teaching. You can find lesson plans for many of our titles at ctpub.com or contact us at ctinfo@ctpub.com.

 For your convenience, we post an up-to-date listing of corrections on our website (ctpub.com and judymartin.com). If a correction is not already posted, please contact Crosley-Griffith Publishing at info@judymartin.com/P.O.Box 512, Grinnell, IA 50112.

Sparkler was pieced by Doris Hareland and quilted by Cindy Kujawa of Cindy's Stitches.

Starlight Medallion was pieced by Sherry McConnell, Stephanie Crabtree, Alyce Taylor, and Cathy Goins and quilted by Linda Lupton, all of The Quilting Collective.

American Hero was pieced by Marilyn Deppe and quilted by Carol Westercamp.

Stars Over the States was pieced by Tammie Klein and Neil Thompson and quilted by John Kerstein of 2 Guyz Quilting.

Shakespeare in the Park in queen size was pieced by Judy Martin and quilted by Debbi Treusch.

Shakespeare in the Park in twin size was pieced by Margy Sieck and quilted by Jean Nolte.

The Red, White & Blue was pieced by Mary Bird and quilted by Vicki Bales.

July Fireworks was pieced by Chris Hulin and quilted by Carol Westercamp.

Rise & Shine in red, white and blue was pieced and quilted by Sally Yakish.

Rise & Shine in blue and white was pieced by Judy Martin and quilted by Debbi Treusch.

Stars 'n' Stripes Forever was pieced by Mary Bird and quilted by Vicki Bales.

Star-Spangled Quilt tops in 2 sizes were pieced by Marilyn Deppe and quilted by Carol Westercamp.

Star Bright was pieced by Chris Hulin and quilted by Carol Westercamp.

Stars in Stripes was pieced by Chris Hulin and quilted by Carol Westercamp.

Paul Revere's Ride was pieced by Mary Bird and quilted by Vicki Bales.

O Beautiful! was pieced by Tracey Barber of Lyons Quilting and quilted by Donna Smith.

America, the Beautiful was pieced by Judy Martin and quilted by Jean Nolte.

Military Band was pieced by Judy Martin and quilted by Debbi Treusch.

I offer many thanks to the quilt makers who contributed their time and talents to make the quilts in this book. I thank my son, Will Bennett, for designing America, the Beautiful and for helping to prepare photography for printing. I also wish to thank my husband, Steve Bennett, for his incomparable proofreading skills and his input in shaping the contents of this book.

I dedicate this book to America's heroes.

For free downloads to help you rotary cut the prisms, half prisms, and half trapezoids in July Fireworks, Star Spangled Quilt, and O Beautiful! patterns, go to the *Red, White & Blue Star Quilts* Extras page at judymartin.com

On this page, you will also find free downloads for trimming points, links to viewer photos, class outlines, and any errata related to the book.

About the Author

Red, White & Blue Star Quilts: 16 Striking Patriotic and 2-Color Patterns is Judy Martin's 28th book since 1980. She is a prolific designer of traditional-style quilts intended for intermediate to advanced quilt makers. She specializes in scrap quilts, star quilts, Log Cabin variations, pieced borders, and new block and setting designs. She has also written two books of useful charts for quilt makers: *Taking the Math Out of Making Patchwork Quilts* in 1981 and *Judy Martin's Ultimate Rotary Cutting Reference* in 1997.

Judy has designed and published 1269 patterns for original blocks and quilts during her 8 years as an editor at *Quilter's Newsletter* and *Quiltmaker* magazines and 34 subsequent years of self-publishing books and patterns. This is her first book published by C & T Publishing.

Judy still gets a thrill from seeing an idea developed into a computer drawing, interpreted in fabric, and transformed into a quilt at her sewing machine. She hopes that you will get a similar thrill seeing your time, effort, and fabric choices transform her designs into your own quilt vision.

Sparkler, page 22

Star-Spangled Quilt, p. 66

Rise & Shine, page 54

Sparkler, page 26

Star-Spangled Quilt, p. 66

Stars Over the States, page 34

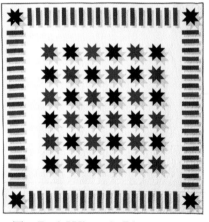

The Red, White & Blue, page 46

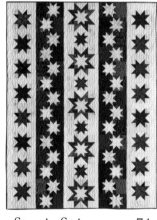

Stars in Stripes, page 74

Military Band, page 92

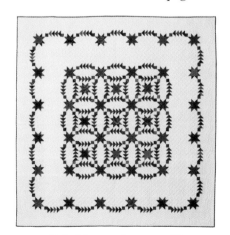

July Fireworks, page 50

Stars 'n' Stripes Forever, p. 62

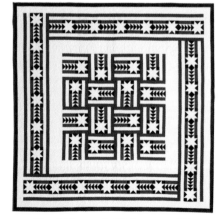

Paul Revere's Ride, page 78

TABLE OF CONTENTS

Rise & Shine, page 57

O Beautiful!, page 81

American Hero, page 31

Star Bright, page 70

Shakespeare in the Park, page 38

America, the Beautiful, p. 88

Shakespeare in the Park, page 42

Starlight Medallion, page 27

INTRODUCTION

High-contrast color schemes of red and white, blue and white, and red, white and blue are enduring favorites for good reason. The colors schemes are bold, yet timeless. The straightforward contrasts are easily mastered by a beginning quilt maker. The quilts look equally stunning in all-over scraps or 2 solid fabrics. Pairing classic Evening Stars and Rising Stars with these color schemes makes perfect sense: Both the color plans and the geometric forms contribute to the simple beauty. The stars are striking in their spikey silhouettes and bright colors yet comforting in their familiarity. These are basic stars, made from common shapes. Still, set in new arrangements with curved illusions, refreshing asymmetry, or unique combinations of several types and sizes of blocks, these stars sparkle anew.

When the pandemic arrived, I needed a project. I have always loved quilts in classic 2-color schemes of red and white or blue and white, and I felt compelled to explore them further. Red, white and blue quilts, with their strong contrasts, seemed a natural extension. In my computer files of designs yet to be published, I found my inspiration in a couple of designs using basic stars in new settings. I tweaked them, named them Stars Over the States and American Hero, and had the beginnings of a book.

My old books yielded a couple of favorite out-of-print patterns fitting this theme, so I added my patriotic quilt, Stars 'n' Stripes Forever and my 2-color classic, Shakespeare in the Park.

The rest of the book developed organically. My next design is usually based on an idea sparked by one of my previous designs. Inspired by the circles in Stars Over the States, I arranged small Evening Stars and larger Rising Stars in concentric circles to create Military Band. I took my Star Cluster B.O.M. to another level by surrounding the block with the same motif at four times the size to create Sparkler. For Rise & Shine, I fashioned sashing from Evening Stars to frame the Rising Star blocks. For Stars in Stripes I combined several borders from other quilts in the book to make a strippy quilt. One thing led to another, and soon I had 16 quilt designs.

This book includes patterns for 16 quilts and 7 size and color variations. I illustrate 24 additional colorings for these patterns on pages 18–21, 25, 29, 39, 44, 52, 68, 76, and 89. I tell you how to easily convert the cutting lists and yardage amounts for 20

of the variations. It's a simple matter of swapping one color for another or adding 2 yardage figures and cutting lists together. Doing so lets you make 2 more patriotic quilts and 18 additional 2-color quilts from these 16 patriotic and seven 2-color patterns. A bit of figuring, will give you 4 more.

Charts on page 17 listing yardage for Evening Stars or Rising Stars will assist you in altering the patterns in these last 4 examples. Another chart on page 16 lists patch cutting dimensions for a range of Rising Star and Evening Star block sizes. These charts will come in handy should you desire to design your own star quilts.

I planned the diagrams and specifications boxes to lead you visually through every step of making the quilts, with a minimum of words.

General quilt making information and specific helps for making Rising Stars and Evening Stars are on pages 8–15 to provide additional support.

Patterns here range from a quick little table topper to king-sized quilts: 5 patterns are wall sized, 7 are throw or twin sized, and 11 are queen to king sized. Official Quilts of Valor® measure 55" x 65" to 72" x 90", with 60" x 80" recommended. I present 6 patriotic patterns in this size range: American Hero; The Red, White & Blue; Rise & Shine; Stars 'n' Stripes Forever; Star-Spangled Quilt; and Stars in Stripes.

Many of us have stories behind our patriotic quilts. Here's my story: Both of my parents served in the U.S. Navy during World War II. My dad was still in the Navy when I was in grade school, and having grown up military, it was only natural that I designed a quilt when I was processing the events of September 11, 2001. Stars 'n' Stripes Forever was my 9/11 quilt, and my then-ten-year-old son, Will, joined me, designing his America, the Beautiful quilt that same day. I have designed other patriotic quilts over the years. In fact, my first quilt in 1969 was one of them. I designed my most recent quilt, Military Band, specifically to honor my dad. That starry border just looks to me like horns blaring out a Sousa march.

Whatever the story is behind your patriotic quilt, whether you are sewing for Quilts of Valor® or honoring a loved one privately, I hope you find inspiration in this volume. And if your taste runs to graphic 2-color quilts, I show all but one of the patriotic quilts in 2 colors, as well. I hope you have as much fun making these quilts as I had designing them!

READ THIS PAGE
IF YOU HAVE ANY QUESTIONS ABOUT THE PATTERNS

My designs are unique, and my patterns and method are likely a bit different, as well. I chose my method initially because I have been writing books since the days of templates. When rotary cutting was new, many quilt makers were still using templates. **Rotary cutting patches** allowed me to present a single set of instructions for **machine piecing** for use with either cutting technique. I continue using this method because it is straightforward, it works for just about any pattern, and the scrap placement possibilities are maximized. (Almost all of the quilts that I make are scrap quilts.) Unlike quilts that use paper piecing, strip piecing, or flip-and-sew techniques, my method remains the same for different designs. Furthermore, when you cut through four layers, the efficiency exceeds most shortcuts. If you have a favorite method for making Flying Geese units or Four-Patches, feel free to use it, but understand that you may need a little more yardage than I allowed, due to the likelihood of leftover strip ends or other waste. Rotary-cutting patches allows you to cut shapes well beyond the squares, rectangles, and right triangles that most shortcuts address. Most of the shapes in these patterns are basic ones, but a few of the patterns utilize prisms, half prisms, trapezoids, or half trapezoids, as well.

I do not allow extra for trimming down units or squaring up blocks, as these are unnecessary and wasteful steps once you have taken a few moments to master your seam allowances.

I list the exact dimensions for border strips, including seam allowances (but without any extra for insurance). Usually when a quilt does not come out the listed size, it is slightly shy of it, so my exact borders are more than sufficient. If you think it likely that your quilt will turn out larger than expected, add a little to the listed border length.

These patterns were designed to provide **everything you need at a glance.** Yardage and cutting dimensions are listed in a specifications box, and every detail of block and quilt construction is shown in plentiful diagrams. The narrative is minimal, including caveats and special details, along with brief coverage of the basics. **On pages 12–13, I present step-by-step narrative directions for making the Rising Star and Evening Star blocks** that are used throughout the book.

Block and quilt diagrams are exploded to varying degrees to show the sewing progression. Patches that are touching within the most exploded areas are joined first, followed by elements that are separated by the narrowest margins. Parts that are farthest apart are sewn last. Usually, a block or quilt has repeating elements, and in each half, quarter, or row I show one part nearly completely exploded, and others less exploded. Occasionally, I show a separate, numbered piecing diagram, where you add patches in numerical order.

Though I show diagrams of whole blocks, you need not make one block at a time. Feel free to use **assembly-line techniques.** You can easily see the construction units in the exploded diagrams. That said, I find it more interesting and just as fast to chain piece two blocks at a time rather than sewing all the Flying Geese units at once.

Though the specifications box, with its cutting list, is presented at the start of a pattern, **you do not have to cut out the entire quilt before you start sewing.** In fact, I recommend you begin by cutting just enough to sew a block or two to test your fabric choices and sewing accuracy. After that, it's up to you. I know I am always anxious to see what the quilt is going to look like, so I may test one or two of each type of block before finishing the cutting. If I am making the kind of scrap quilt that uses just a handful of fabrics within a block, but many different sets of fabrics overall, I may cut enough fabric for just a block or two at a time throughout the quilt-making process.

Besides the cutting lists, the specifications box presents patch, block, star, and quilt sizes, block and unit quantities, and yardage requirements. Block, star, and quilt dimensions are finished sizes, not including seam allowances. Patch dimensions are cut sizes, with seam allowances included. Patches are listed by color in size order, with the largest patches first. **Cut borders and large patches first and cut smaller ones from leftovers.**

Yardage figures allow 5% extra for shrinkage, in case you prewash your fabric. Additionally, I allow a little extra for the occasional cutting error.

Backing includes seams plus 8" extra. The extra is helpful for longarmers, but you can scale it back if you quilt by hand or by home sewing machine.

STELLAR TIPS

The star quilts in this book are within your grasp, whether you think so or not. When I was writing my book, *Stellar Quilts,* the first thing I did was to recruit a beginner to test my premise that anyone could master a star. My neighbor Anne, who loves quilts and had only made a baby quilt of basic squares, was the perfect candidate. I spent a few minutes showing her my block and giving her a few pointers. Then I gave her a handful of fat quarters and a pattern for a star block. A short time later Anne showed off her perfect block, proclaiming it the most beautiful thing she had ever made.

IT JUST SEAMS RIGHT

Anne had a leg up when she made her perfect star block because she was using my sewing machine. My machine already had a tape guide in place for a perfect scant ¼" seam allowance. I have always maintained that you can sew anything once you master the seam allowance. Mastering your seam allowance will take a half hour of your time and serve you well for the rest of your quilt-making years. If your patchwork results have been less than stellar in the past, deal with your seam allowance before you start your next project.

The perfect seam allowance has nothing to do with measuring your seam allowance. Instead, you determine it by sewing a sample with several seams and comparing that sample to an unstitched patch. Start by rotary cutting nine 1½" squares and a 1½" x 9½" rectangle. Join the squares end to end. Press seams to one side. Place the rectangle and squares face to face. If the seamed squares turned out smaller than the rectangle, your seams are too deep; if the rectangle is smaller, your seams are too shallow. Say your seamed unit is ¼" too small. You have taken eight seams, with each seam affecting the finished size of two squares. That means each seam allowance is too deep by ¹⁄₆₄" (¼" ÷ 16). If you even have a ruler with ¹⁄₆₄" rulings, your eyes are better than mine if you can keep the marks from running together. This line is ¹⁄₆₄" wide and 1½" long: ▬▬▬▬▬▬▬▬▬
It doesn't look like much, but it can add up to 2"–4" in a quilt, depending on the patch and quilt size. Your adjustment will probably be very small, just the width of one or two threads. I mark my seam allowance with a piece of black electrical tape on the throatplate of my sewing machine. It leaves a slight ridge to follow, and it doesn't get as gummy as masking tape. My machine has a line etched on the throatplate that is supposedly a ¼" seam allowance. It is too deep, but it provides a nice line parallel to which I can run the tape. After applying the tape, make a second sample with the adjusted seam allowance. Repeat as needed until your sample is perfect.

Take a few moments to master your seam allowance. Get it right, and save time and aggravation later when your patchwork fits together effortlessly!

THE WHYS AND WISE OF LENGTHWISE GRAIN

The lengthwise grain is parallel to the selvage. It is the least stretchy grain. It is more stable than the crosswise grain, and it follows the printed pattern more closely. While squares and half-square triangles will have sides on both lengthwise and crosswise grains, starting with the lengthwise grain is a good habit, nonetheless. For rectangles and other long shapes, you want the longer sides on the lengthwise grain for stability. For diamonds, where two sides are on the straight grain and two are on the bias, you want to follow the lengthwise grain rather than crosswise for a less stretchy edge.

THE POINT OF POINT TRIMMING

The main point of trimming points is to help you align the ends of neighboring patches with each other before stitching. Eliminating bulk and dogears in the seams is just a bonus. For 45° angles, such as those in ¼- and ½-square triangles and other shapes in this book, my Point Trimmer tool works perfectly.

TRIMMING POINTS USING A REGULAR RULER OR A GUIDE

If you don't have my Point Trimmer, you can download a file of charts and instructions for using a regular ruler to trim points. You can also download a file with guides you can print, cut out, and affix to your ruler. Both downloads are available by going to the RWB Extras page at judymartin.com

Most of the common patches, such as squares and rectangles, are symmetrical; that is, they look the same face up or face down. These can be cut right- or left-handed, with fabric folded in half or not, with the same results. Some other patches, such as long triangles, parallelograms, and half trapezoids, are asymmetrical. Take special care to cut these asymmetrical patches according to your quilt plan.

Some quilts call for asymmetrical patches and their reverses in equal quantities. These are mirror images; cut both at the same time from fabric folded in half.

Mirror images can also be cut from stacked fat quarters that are not folded. Arrange half of them face up and half face down in the stack.

Sometimes all asymmetrical patches in a quilt are alike. In such a case, you must not fold the fabric. Furthermore, care must be taken to keep stacked fabrics all facing the same side up.

Use fabric that is face up to cut patches that do not have an "r" after the patch letter. Use fabric that is face down to cut their reverses, indicated wth an "r" following the patch letter.

LOSE YOUR ANTI-BIAS BIAS

Stars have points, and that means triangles and bias edges. The bias grain is really no big deal. You are not likely to stretch it as long as it is flat on a table or against the bed of your sewing machine. Actually, bias is nothing to fear once your seam allowance is right. Most stretching comes from over-handling fabric, especially when you rip seams. You won't have nearly so much seam ripping when you have mastered your seam allowances.

Other factors that can neutralize the bias threat include point trimming, pinning, and finger pressing. If you trim points, you can see exactly how patches

are supposed to align with their neighbors. If your seam allowance is perfect, you can trust the fit. If you pin seams and joints, you can keep things properly aligned. If you finger press instead of using an iron (at least until the bias edge is seamed) you can avoid stretching bias edges. And if you don't push or pull fabric as you stitch, but gently guide your fabric along your seam guide as the patches lie flat on the sewing machine bed, you are not going to stretch anything out of shape.

Now, repeat after me: "Bias is no big deal." Relax; you've got this.

PIN-POINT PRECISION

For precise sewing, rely on pins. Most sewing machines do not feed the top and bottom fabrics evenly. Pins can keep joints aligned as you stitch. I pin at every joint and at intervals of 3" or less on long seams when joining rows of blocks, attaching borders, or stitching together backing panels. Pinning also helps when you are working with bias edges. If you have trimmed points, it is easy to align the ends of the seam. Pinning the seam at both ends will give you results you can count on. You may find that laying

your work on a flat surface helps you keep it flat and even while you pin. If you are pinning with the work on a bed or ironing board, slip a cutting mat under the patchwork so you don't pin through to the bed covers or ironing board pad.

I like short, fine pins with small heads. I leave the pins in place at the joints and stitch over them. Larger pins make a bigger hump to waddle over. The fine pins bend easily, but they are inexpensive, and I keep an extra box on hand.

THE WHOLE POINT

Sharp points define a good star. Don't miss the point by cutting yours off with less-than-stellar sewing. Mastering your seam allowance will go a long way toward assuring good points. Realizing that the points are supposed to be ¼" in from the raw edge will help, as well. At a point, your seam allowances

should cross in an "X," with the intersection ¼" in from the cut edge. If your stitching line goes across the intersection, perfect joints are assured. Your star points will be sharp and precisely on the edge of the block after the last seams are taken: those stitching the blocks into rows and the rows into the quilt.

PRESSING MATTERS

Be careful not to stretch bias edges out of shape when you press. Use a dry iron and press only in the direction of the straight grain of the fabric. It is not necessary to press after each seam. You can simply

finger press the seam allowances to one side from the right side of the fabric. Use common sense when deciding which way to press seam allowances. You don't want dark seam allowances to show through

9

PRESSING MATTERS, *continued*

light patches; you don't want too much bulk in any one place; and you don't want a patch to billow because all of its seam allowances are pressed toward the patch. Furthermore, you do want seams to oppose at joints. That is, you want the seam allowance pressed to one side for one unit and pressed to the opposite side on the other unit. Each seam will form a ridge, and when you slide one unit next to the other, you can feel the two seam allowances locking together when they are precisely aligned. The first rule of pressing is to press away from the bulk. That

is, if you are sewing a single patch to a seamed unit, press the seam allowances toward the single patch. Where many points come together, press all seam allowances clockwise (or all counter-clockwise) so that they will oppose each other. Even if it means pressing toward the bulk, press at least one seam of every patch away from the patch.

When the bias edges are all stitched or blocks are complete, you can use a steam iron. Steam is particularly useful when pressing toward the bulk. Also use steam afer joining blocks into rows and joining rows.

LET YOUR FINGERS DO THE PRESSING

As you sew the patches together for your quilt, crease the seams to one side using your thumbnail rather than using an iron. I lay the unit, right side up, on my thigh. I run my thumbnail along the seam line to train the seam allowance in the right direction. I prefer my thumbnail to a pressing stick. It lets

me feel the seam to make sure it is fully open. I press my fabric before cutting patches, and I may not press again with an iron until the bias edges are stitched. Careful finger pressing won't stretch bias. It prevents tucks and preserves the ridges of the seam allowances to make perfectly matched joints a breeze.

Y-SEAMS? WHY NOT?

Set-in seams or Y-seams (indicated by a pink dot in the diagrams) are used in just one of the patterns here: Rise & Shine. If you cut and stitch accurately, your set-in patches will fall into place naturally. The important thing to remember about set-in patches is that you must not stitch over the seam allowances at the joint. The seam allowances need to be free in

order for the joint to lie flat. You will have to stitch a Y-seam in two passes: from the joint to one end and from the joint to the other end. You must not pivot at the joint to continue stitching. Start the first line of stitching ¼" in from the raw edge at the joint. For the second pass, remove the work from the machine and stitch from the joint to the other end.

ARE YOU PARTIAL TO PARTIAL SEAMS?

Partial seams are used when a joint is crossed by a straight seam, but you need to make the seam in two passes because one of the two segments you are joining extends beyond the other. These seams are easy to do. You simply start sewing at the end of the seam where the segments are even with each other, but you stop sewing before you get to the uneven end.

Often, the partial seam will allow you to take regular seams next. When you get further along, and the two segments are now even, you may complete the partial seam, stitching from where you stopped before to the end of the seam line.

In this book, I indicate a partial seam with a green dashed line between two green dots.

BACKING A WINNER

The backing sizes listed in my patterns allow the extra 8" of length and width required for mounting on a longarm quilting machine. Unless your quilt is very small or you are using extra-wide backing material, you will have to join two or three lengths of material to make your backing. Trim the selvages off the yard goods before cutting out the panels. Cut out the quilt panels as listed in the pattern. (I list backing yardage from 45"-wide fabric. If you are using

108"-wide backing fabric, cut one piece in the quilt dimensions plus 8" in length and width.) Make a fresh cut at the end of the length of backing fabric to square it up. Use a square ruler or a long, wide one to make sure the corners are square. Cut each panel precisely the same length and width. Pin and stitch panels together with ¼" seam allowances. Press seam allowances to one side. Press the quilt top and backing well. Pick off or snip any stray threads.

PREPARATION & QUILTING

Press your completed quilt top and snip or pick off stray threads. You are now ready to deliver your quilt and backing to your trusted longarm quilter. Consider taking this book along for quilting suggestions.

If you plan to quilt the top yourself, I cannot teach you hand- or machine-quilting in the space of a few paragraphs. I suggest you take a class or get a book devoted exclusively to that subject. If you are already well versed in quilting, I suggest you study the block photographs on page 14 to give you some quilting ideas. In the quilts that I pieced, I had all of the stars quilted in the ditch around their points to add definition. My quilter also used ruler work and freehand feathers extensively.

BOUND FOR GLORY

In preparation for binding, use a rotary cutter and ruler to trim the batting and backing even with the quilt top. Take special care to achieve right angles at the corners. Cut the binding fabric into straight strips (or bias) 2" wide and in sufficient quantity to go around the quilt's perimeter with several inches to spare. Trim the ends of the strips at a 45° angle, with all ends parallel to one another when the strips are all right side up. Trim the points using my Point Trimmer's A trim to help you align the strips for seaming. Pin and stitch the strips end to end with ¼" seam allowances to make one long strip. Press these seam allowances open. Fold the strip in half lengthwise with right sides out. Press the fold for the full length of the binding strip.

Lay the quilt face up on a flat surface. Starting on one edge of the quilt (and not near the corner), lay the folded binding strip over one edge of the quilt. Start about 4"–6" from one end of the binding. Align the raw edges of the two layers of binding with the cut edges of the quilt top, and pin through both layers of binding plus the quilt top, batting, and backing. Pin and stitch the binding to just one edge of the quilt, stopping ¼" from the raw edge at the corner of the quilt. Wrap the binding around to the back of the quilt at the corner so it is even with the binding on the front. Crease the binding crosswise at the quilt's raw edge. Now bring this creased edge

to the front of the quilt and align the crease with the raw edge of the part you just stitched. Pin at the corner, then pin along the entire next side. Stitch from ¼" from the crease in the binding at one corner to ¼" from the raw edge at the next corner. Backtack at the ends of the seam. Repeat this process until

the binding is stitched to all edges and around all corners. Stop stitching 8"–10" short of your starting point. Lay the starting end of the binding strip over the quilt top, and pin it to the edge of the quilt ¼" from the binding's starting end.

Lay the final end of the binding strip over it. With a pin, mark the point where this strip meets the pin at the end of the first strip. I always position this pin to follow the angle at the end of the first strip. This pin marks the seam line joining the two strip ends.

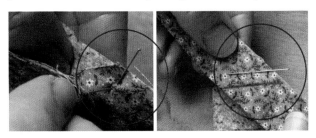

Unfold and cut off the end strip ¼" outside the pin at a 45° angle. Trim the point using the A trim of my Point Trimmer. Pin the two binding strip ends together and stitch with a ¼" seam. Press seams open. Refold the binding in half lengthwise and pin it to the quilt. Stitch from the point where you left off to the starting point, backtacking at both ends.

Wrap the binding around the perimeter of the quilt to the back side as you hand stitch. Align the crease with the stitching line that attached the binding strip. Hem stitch by hand to secure the binding to the back of the quilt. At the corners, stitch to the end of the stitching line. Position the binding for the beginning of the next side. Take a stitch to secure the binding for the next side to the corner, and use your needle to tuck under the excess at the miter. Continue until the binding is hand stitched all around.

CUTTING THE BLOCKS

For our cutting examples, we'll consider a 6" Evening Star and a 12" Rising Star.

The Evening Star has patches of 4 types: 1 A square, 8 B half-square triangles, 4 C quarter-square triangles, and 4 D squares.

A) See figure 1. Cut A squares from 3½"-wide strips that you further cut into 3½" squares.

B) See figure 2. Cut the B half-square triangles from 2⅜"-wide strips that you cut into 2⅜" squares. Then cut each square in half diagonally to make 2 triangles, as shown in figure 2.

C) See figure 3. Cut the C quarter-square triangles from 4¼"-wide strips. Cut the strips into 4¼" squares. Then cut each square in half along both diagonals to make 4 triangles, making both cuts before moving the patches.

D) See figure 1. Cut the D squares from 2"-wide strips that you further cut into 2" squares.

The Rising Star has an Evening Star center and additional patches of 3 types: 8 E half-square triangles, 4 F quarter-square triangles, and 4 more A squares that you cut the same way you cut the A in the Evening Star block.

A) Cut additional A squares as shown in figure 1. Cut 3½"-wide strips; further cut the strips into 3½" squares. These may be a different color from the A in the center of the Evening Star.

E) See figure 2. Cut the E half-square triangles from 3⅞"-wide strips that you cut into 3⅞" squares. Then cut each square in half diagonally to make 2 triangles.

F) See figure 3. Cut the F quarter-square triangles from 7¼"-wide strips that you cut into 7¼" squares. Then cut each square in half along both diagonals to make 4 triangles, making both cuts before moving the patches.

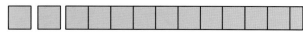

Figure 1. Rotary cut strips of the listed width. Use the same measurement to cut squares from each strip.

Fig. 2. Cut each square in half diagonally to make 2 triangles with straight grain on the 2 short sides.

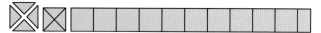

Figure 3. Cut each square in half along both diagonals to make 4 triangles with straight grain on the long side.

Trim ½-square triangle points using the A trim of my Point Trimmer; use the B trim for ¼-square triangles. Download a point trimming file from judymartin.com

PIECING THE EVENING STAR

Evening Star

Step 1: Unit 1
make 4
"V" arrows indicate the direction to press seam allowances.

Step 2: Rows 1 and 3
make 2

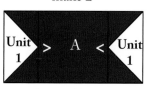

Step 3: Row 2
make 1

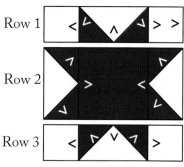

Step 4: Evening Star Block Piecing

Step 1: Sew 2 B triangles to a C triangle. Press seams away from the C. Make 4 of these units.

Step 2: Add a D square to each end of a unit from step 1. Press seams toward the D's to complete row 1. Repeat for row 3.

Step 3: Sew the 2 remaining units from step 1 to opposite sides of an A square to complete row 2. Press seam allowances toward the A square.

Step 4: Join rows 1–3 as shown to complete the block. Press seams away from the center row.

PIECING THE RISING STAR

Rising Star

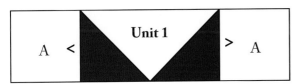

Step 2: Rows 1 and 3
make 2

Step 3: Row 2
make 1

Note that color placement varies in Evening Stars and Rising Stars from different patterns in this book.

"V" arrows indicate the direction to press the seam allowances.

At the center of the Rising Star block is an Evening Star block, shown on the previous page.

Points are not at the edges until all seams are sewn. I do not show the seam allowances in these diagrams.

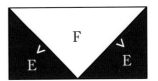

Step 1: Unit 1
make 4

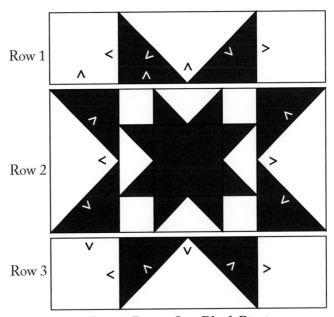

Step 4: Rising Star Block Piecing

Step 1: Sew 2 E triangles to an F triangle. Press seams away from the F. Make 4 of these unit 1's.

Step 2: Add an A square to each end of a unit 1. Press seams toward the A's to complete row 1. Repeat for row 3.

Step 3: Make an Evening Star block for the center of the block, as shown on the previous page. Add the 2 remaining units from step 1 to opposite sides of the Evening Star block. Steam press seam allowances away from the center block to complete row 2.

Step 4: Join rows 1, 2, and 3 in numerical order, as shown above. Note that the seam allowances of rows 1 and 2 and those of rows 2 and 3 do not oppose. I recommend flipping one seam to oppose and pinning the seam allowance that you did not flip. Then flip the other seam allowance back to its original pressing direction and insert a second pin. Stitch the seams and press seam allowances away from the Evening Star center to complete the Rising Star block as shown above.

DETAILS: FABRICS & QUILTING

A classic 2-color quilt can be made from 2 prints, 2 solids, or a variety of scraps sorted into 2 colors. For patriotic quilts you sort into 3 colors, so the range is a bit tighter. Solids tend toward simplicity and a graphic quality. Scraps tend toward busyness and nuance. I like the many little creative decisions that come from using scraps. My preference for quilting is to accentuate the stars wth in-the-ditch or outline quilting. I like feathers and curves in the background to contrast with the straight lines in the stars.

I chose very subtly printed light scraps paired with red prints that ranged more in hue and pattern. Feathers and straight-line quilting were done by Debbi Treusch.

I chose navy scraps that read as solids and busier cream prints. Debbi Treusch quilted the stars in the ditch and in straight lines and filled the background with feathers.

Here, I chose subtly printed, nearly solid light scraps, pairing them with somewhat busier navy prints. Debbi Treusch quilted a feathered circle in the background.

Doris Hareland chose contemporary scraps for the red and blue and a single white background fabric. Cindy Kujawa quilted the white with freehand curves.

SPECIAL ROTARY CUTTING

Using the Shapemaker 45 to Cut Special Shapes

The Shapemaker 45 (S45) is my multi-purpose rotary cutting ruler. It is useful for rotary cutting the nested half trapezoids, prisms, and half prisms in this book and many other shapes, as well. These diagrams and instructions are for cutting the shapes in this book using the S45.

If you do not have an S45, download a file by going to the RWB Extras page at judymartin.com

Using the Shapemaker 45 to Cut Half Trapezoids

For H and Hr half trapezoids from O Beautiful!, see the diagram below. Start by cutting a stack of 2 rectangles measuring 2⅝"x 7⅝" from folded fabric. Align the bottom of the tool with one long edge of the rectangle stack. Align the 5⅛" ruling with the left short end of the rectangle. Cut along the ruler's angled edge to make 2 H and 2 Hr.

Rotary Cutting H & Hr Half Trapezoids for O Beautiful! with Shapemaker 45

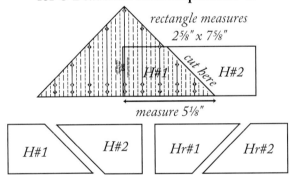

rectangle measures 2⅝" x 7⅝"

cut here

H#1   H#2

measure 5⅛"

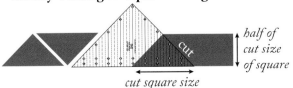

H#1   H#2   Hr#1   Hr#2

cut H face up and Hr face down in a stack

Using the S45 to Rotary Cut ¼-Square Triangles

The S45 gives you the option to cut ¼-square triangles all on the same grain without cutting a square. Cut a strip in a width *half* the cut size listed for the square. Cut off the strip end at a 45° angle. Align the S45's long side with the long edge of the strip as you align the ruling for the square's listed cut size with the strip's point. Cut along the S45's angled edge to complete a triangle. Turn the strip face down to cut the next triangle, measuring from the new point.

Rotary Cutting ¼-Square Triangles with S45

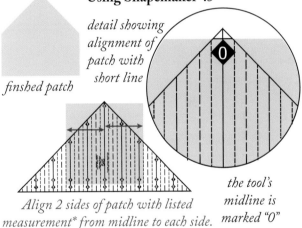

half of cut size of square

cut

cut square size

Using the Shapemaker 45 to Rotary Cut Prisms & Half Prisms

For prisms and half prisms in 3 patterns in this book, see the diagram and chart below. Cut a square or rectangle in the dimensions listed for your patch. Align the short line near the top of the S45 with the short end of the rectangle or the top of the square, as shown. Align the listed measurement* on each side of the tool's midline, which is marked "0," with the sides of the square or long sides of the rectangle. Cut off the 2 triangles that extend above the S45. Repeat at the opposite end if your patch has 2 pointy ends.

If you do not have an S45 tool, you can download a paper guide to cut out and tape to a rotary ruler for rotary cutting each of the special shapes in this book. Find the guides, along with complete instructions, by going to the RWB Extras page at judymartin.com

Rotary Cutting Prisms & Half Prisms Using Shapemaker 45

detail showing alignment of patch with short line

finshed patch

Align 2 sides of patch with listed measurement* from midline to each side.

the tool's midline is marked "0"

Prisms & Half Prisms: Cut Size of Sq./Rectangle & Measurement* from Midline to Each Side

Name	Patch	Sq./Rect.	Meas.*/#ends
July Fireworks	E	3½" x 12½"	1¾"/2 ends
July Fireworks	G	3½" x 3½"	1¾"/1 end
Star-Spangled	E	4½" x 4½"	2¼"/1 end
O Beautiful!	L	6½" x 27½"	3¼"/2 ends
O Beautiful!	M	6½" x 27½"	3¼"/1 end

BLOCK SIZE & CUTTING CHART

Patch Cutting Size for Evening Stars/Rising Stars of Various Finished Sizes

Block Size (finished) Eve./Rising	A □ square Cut Size	B ◹ half-sq. triangle Cut Size	C ⊠ quarter-sq. triangle Cut Size	D □ square Cut Size	E ◹ half-sq. triangle Cut Size	F ⊠ quarter-sq. triangle Cut Size
4"/8"	2½"	1⅞"	3¼"	1½"	2⅞"	5¼"
4½"/9"	2¾"	2"	3½"	1⅝"	3⅛"	5¾"
5"/10"	3"	2⅛"	3¾"	1¾"	3⅜"	6¼"
6"/12"	3½"	2⅜"	4¼"	2"	3⅞"	7¼"
7"/14"	4"	2⅝"	4¾"	2¼"	4⅜"	8¼"
7½"/15"	4¼"	2¾"	5"	2⅜"	4⅝"	8¾"
8"/16"	4½"	2⅞"	5¼"	2½"	4⅞"	9¼"
9"/18"	5"	3⅛"	5¾"	2¾"	5⅜"	10¼"
10"/20"	5½"	3⅜"	6¼"	3"	5⅞"	11¼"
12"/24"	6½"	3⅞"	7¼"	3½"	6⅞"	13¼"
14"/28"	7½"	4⅜"	8¼"	4"	7⅞"	15¼"
15"/30"	8"	4⅝"	8¾"	4¼"	8⅜"	16¼"
16"/32"	8½"	4⅞"	9¼"	4½"	8⅞"	17¼"
18"/36"	9½"	5⅜"	10¼"	5"	9⅞"	19¼"

Note that Evening Star block sizes and cutting are listed in black. Rising Star block sizes are listed in red; Rising Star cutting includes all patches A–F in red and black. A's are used in the center and corners of the Rising Stars.

Example: What patch sizes are needed for an Evening Star as shown at right in a 6" finished size? Follow the 6"/12" line in the chart above to the right. You need 3½" A's, 2⅜" B's, 4¼" C's, and 2" D's.

Example 2: What patch sizes are needed for a Rising Star as shown at right in a 12" finished size? Follow the 6"/12" line in the chart above to the right. You will need all of the cut sizes listed in both black and red on this line: 3½" A's, 2⅜" B's, 4¼" C's, 2" D's., 3⅞" E's, and 7¼" F's.

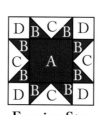

Evening Star

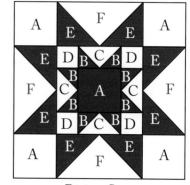

Rising Star

YARDAGE CHARTS FOR STARS
Simply Divide the Number of Blocks You Want by the Number of Blocks per Yard Listed in the Chart

Evening Star　　**Evening Star**

Example: What yardage is needed for 25 blue-and-white Evening Stars as shown above in a 6" size? Figure each color separately. Follow the 6" line in the top chart to the right. From white you can cut 33 blks./yd. You need 25 blocks. Divide 25 by 33. The answer is .76 yards. Look at the bottom chart. .76 rounds up to .875. Follow that decimal to the fraction in the same column: ⅞ yard, your white ydg.

Next, figure the blue yardage. Follow the 6" block line right to the background column: 36 blks./yd. Divide your 25 blocks by 36 = .69 yd., which rounds up to .75 or ¾ yd. in the bottom chart.

Rising Star

Rising Star

Evening Stars: Number of Blocks You Can Cut from a Yard

Star Size (finished)	Stars Fabric 1 A + 8 B per block	Background Fabric 4 C + 4 D per block
4"	63 blocks/yard	60 blocks/yard
5"	45 blocks/yard	44 blocks/yard
6"	33 blocks/yard	36 blocks/yard
8"	22 blocks/yard	21 blocks/yard

12" Rising Stars: Number of Blocks You Can Cut from a Yard

	Number of Blocks Per Yard
Fabric for Small Stars 1 A + 8 B per block	33 blocks/yard
Background Fabric (Sm. Stars) 4 C + 4 D per block	36 blocks/yard
Fabric for Large Stars Points 8 E per block	20 blocks/yard
Background Fabric (Lg. Stars) 4 F + 4 A per block	10 blocks/yard

Converting Decimals to Fractions of Yards

.125	.25	.375	.5	.625	.75	.875
⅛	¼	⅜	½	⅝	¾	⅞

Example: What yardage is needed for 30 blue-and-white Rising Stars as shown at left in a 12" size? Do each color separately. From white you need small stars and large star points. First, follow the line for small stars to the right to 33 blks./yd. Divide your 30 stars by 33 to get .91 yd. Next, follow the Large Star Points line of the chart to the right to 20 blks./yd. Divide your 30 blocks by 20 to get 1.5 yds. Add this to the .91 for the small stars to get 2.41. Referring to the decimal conversion chart, this rounds up to 2.5 or 2½ yds. of white.

Figure blue yardage for small star background and large star background as follows: Divide your 30 blocks by 36 blks./yd. = .83. Also divide 30 blocks by 10 blks./yd. (lg. background) = 3 yds. Add 3 yds. to the .83 = 3.83 and round up to 3⅞ total yds. blue.

CHANGING COLOR SCHEMES:
PATRIOTIC TO 2-COLOR SCHEMES

It's easy to change any of the patriotic schemes in the book to 2 colors. In Rise & Shine, below, simply add together the red and blue yardage figures on page 55. Add the red cutting list to the blue one, and change red to blue in the diagrams. All examples on this page were altered in a similar fashion.

Rise & Shine: *p. 54 substitute navy for red in the diagrams; add the red and navy yardage figures together; add the red cutting list to the navy cutting list.*

July Fireworks: *p. 50, substitute red for navy in diagrams; add the navy and red yardage figures together; add the navy cutting list to the red cutting list.*

Star-Spangled Quilt: *p. 66, substitute red for navy blue in diagrams; add the navy and red yardage figures together; add the navy cutting list to the red cutting list.*

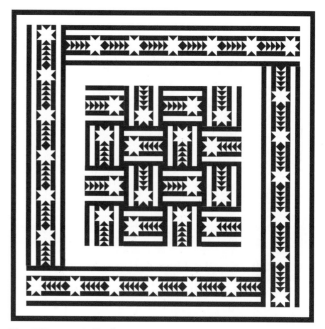

Paul Revere's Ride: *p. 78, substitute navy for red in diagrams; add the red and navy yardage figures together; add the red cutting list to the navy cutting list.*

DIRECTLY SUBSTITUTING HUES & VALUES

The examples below require three hues or values for contrast. The first three examples are new versions of patriotic quilts. The fourth example was originally made in two shades of blue plus cream. All four variations simply exchange one color for another in the yardage, cutting list, and diagrams. The Sparkler quilt on page 22 requires contrast between the red and blue to delineate star points where they touch. The pattern has a slightly lighter red to contrast with the navy. To maintain the contrast in the red-and-white Sparkler here, I chose

dark red and light red (pink). To make this version, simply substitute pink wherever you see navy in the yardage, cutting list, and diagrams.

American Hero and Stars in Stripes, below, keep the values of their patriotic counterparts in the same way. American Hero replaces red wth medium blue. Stars in Stripes replaces red with medium blue and bright blue with navy.

Star Bright goes from two shades of blue plus cream on page 70 to the patriotic scheme shown below by substituting red for medium blue.

Sparkler: *p. 22, substitute pink for navy.*

American Hero: *p. 31, substitute medium blue for red.*

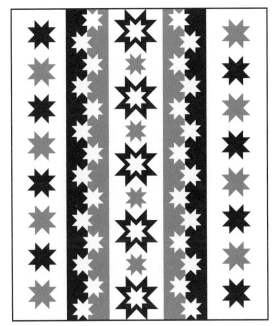

Stars in Stripes: *p. 74, substitute navy for bright blue and medium blue for red.*

Star Bright: *p. 70, substitute red for medium blue.*

DIRECT COLOR SUBSTITUTIONS: ONE QUILT 4 WAYS

Of course, there is more than one way to vary the coloring of these quilts. I present Rise & Shine in one coloring in this chapter and three more starting on page 54. Just to give you an idea of the possibilities in store, on this page, I show four color variations of the patriotic Stars Over the States. Each variation involves a simple substitution. The two examples on the left have two blue values plus cream. To make the first example here, substitute light blue for navy in the yardage, cutting list, and diagrams; similarly substitute navy for white and cream for red.

For the bottom left quilt, replace red with medium blue in the yardage, cutting list and diagrams.

The examples below this column have been converted from 3 colors to 2, so you need to add together yardage figures and cutting lists. In the top quilt, substitute red for white in the yardage, cutting list, and diagrams. Replace both red and blue with cream in the diagrams, and add together the red and blue yardages and cutting lists for the cream total.

In the last quilt, use navy for red in the diagrams and add the red yardage and cutting list to the navy.

Stars Over the States: *p. 34, substitute light blue for navy, navy for white, and cream for red.*

Stars Over the States: *p. 34, substitute red for white; substitute cream for blue and red.*

Stars Over the States: *p. 34, sub med. blue for red.*

Stars Over the States: *p. 34, substitute navy for red.*

20

NOT DIRECT COLOR SUBSTITUTIONS

On this page, I convert 3-color patriotic quilts to 2-color variations and 2-color quilts to patriotic ones. In each case, one color does not replace all of another color, rendering the cutting lists and especially the yardage totals less than helpful. The diagrams involve simple color substitutions within a block or patch, so if you make the quilt from scrap fabrics, one block at a time, you won't need to worry about the yardage and overall patch counts.

The Military Band variation replaces the red in star 2 with cream; it replaces all of the navy with red.

The Stars 'n' Stripes Forever's variation has a bold, graphic simplicity. Replace both red and navy with cream in H, I, and J triangles; also replace the red in the X and Y blocks with navy (E and G patches).

The red-and-white Starlight Medallion changes substantially with the addition of blue. Navy replaces red in the outer pieced and plain borders and in star 2 and blocks U and V. (The star 1 in U remains red.)

Shakespeare in the Park sings a patriotic tune with navy replacing red in Y and Z blocks, in J patches of units 3 and 5, and in star 2.

Military Band: *p. 92, substitute red for navy throughout, and substitute cream for red in star 2.*

Stars 'n' Stripes Forever: *p. 62, substitute cream for red and navy H, I, and J; substitute navy for red E and G.*

Starlight Medallion: *p. 27, substitute navy for red in star 2, red border, blocks V, Y, Z, and U (except its star 1).*

Shakespeare in the Park: *p. 38, substitute navy for red in star 2, blocks Y and Z, and J patches of units 3 and 5.*

21

SPARKLER

Sparkler, 48" x 48", pieced by Doris Hareland and quilted by Cindy Kujawa of Cindy's Stitches. This quilt conveys all the excitement of Independence Day fireworks. The asymmetry of the blocks adds to the flair.

The block in the center of each large star is Star Cluster. I designed it in 2014 as a BOM on my web site. For this book, I recolored the block in patriotic colors and repeated the motif at four times the size for a unique setting.

Select a somewhat light red and a darker navy to contrast with each other where red and blue star points are adjacent. I offer the pattern in a 96" queen size as well as the wall size. Both sizes have the same layout and patch quantities. Patch and border sizes differ.

A version of Sparkler having 2 shades of red plus white is shown on page 19. To make it, you can use the yardage and cutting lists here, simply changing the names of the colors.

With so much negative space in the background, the quilt goes together quickly. You can quilt it simply or gloriously, as you desire.

WALL QUILT SPECIFICATIONS

Quilt Size: 48" x 48"
Block Size: 8" W blocks, 32" X block,
  4" Y & Z blocks
Star Sizes: 4" and 16"
Requires: 8 unit 1, 8 unit 2, 2 unit 3,
  2 unit 4, 4 W, 1 X, 10 Y, 10 Z

YARDAGE & CUTTING

½ yard or 3 fat qtrs. ea. of Navy & Red:
(from each color cut the following)
16 E ◹ half-square triangles cut from
  8 squares cut 4⅞"
18 A ☐ squares cut 2½"
144 B ◹ half-square triangles cut from
  72 squares cut 1⅞"

2½ yards White or Cream:
2 borders* cut 2½" x 48½"
2 borders* cut 2½" x 44½"
2 borders* cut 2½" x 36½"

White or Cream: *continued*

2 borders* cut 2½" x 32½"
8 I ▭ rectangles* cut 4½" x 16½"
8 F ⊠ quarter-square triangles cut from
  2 squares cut 9¼"
8 E ◹ half-square triangles cut from
  4 squares cut 4⅞"
4 G ☐ squares cut 4½"
32 H ▭ rectangles* cut 1½" x 4½"
112 C ⊠ quarter-square triangles cut
  from 28 squares cut 3¼"
32 B ◹ half-square triangles cut from
  16 squares cut 1⅞"
96 D ☐ squares cut 1½"

3⅜ yards 44"-Wide Backing Fabric:
2 panels cut 28½" x 56½"

½ yard Binding Fabric:
2" x 202"

Yardage and cutting for navy and red are identical. Buy ½ yard of navy and ½ yard of red. Cut the listed patches from each color.

Note that the wall quilt uses the same patch letters, diagrams, and instructions as the queen quilt. The patch dimensions and border lengths differ. Use the specifications here for the wall quilt. Use the quantities and diagrams on page 24–25 for both sizes. The whole quilt diagram for the wall size is on page 25.

*Rotary cut H and I rectangles and borders with the long edges on the lengthwise grain of the fabric.

Be sure to read the material at the front of the book that explains my method, identifies exactly what I include in my dimensions and yardage figures, teaches you how to get the most out of the diagrams, and details how to rotary cut and piece the Evening Star blocks.

Rotary cut the longest borders first, cutting parallel to the selvage. Then cut the shorter borders and the largest patches. The specifications box lists the largest patches first. Cut smaller patches from the leftovers. Cut all rectangles with their long edges parallel to the selvage.

You need not cut everything before you start sewing. You can cut a little and sew a little, if you like. If you plan to do that, start by cutting off a length sufficient for the borders and set it aside. Next, cut I and H rectangles. Then use the remainder of the white or cream to cut the patches you intend to sew first.

If you wish, eliminate dogears by trimming the points of the B, C, E, and F triangles. Use the A trim of my Point Trimmer for B and E triangles and the B trim for C and F triangles. If you prefer, download instructions for using a regular ruler to trim points from the RWB Extras page at judymartin.com

SPARKLER BLOCKS & UNITS FOR 2 SIZES

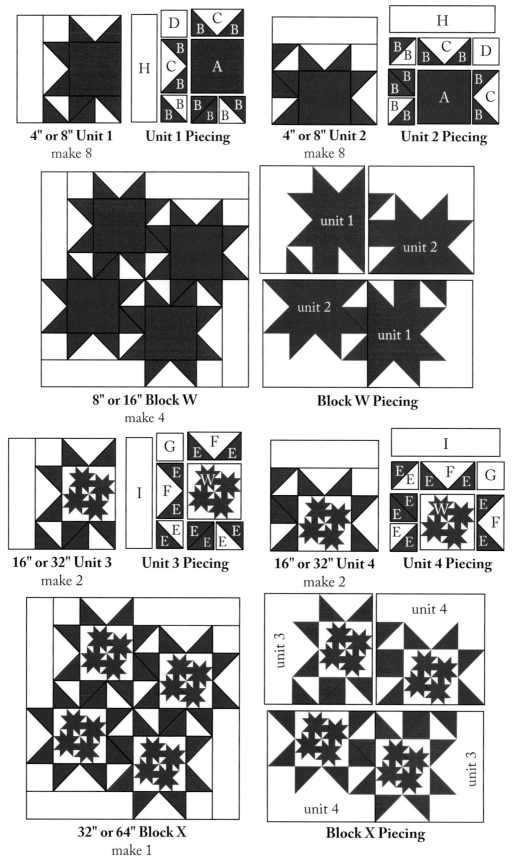

4" or 8" Unit 1
make 8

Unit 1 Piecing

4" or 8" Unit 2
make 8

Unit 2 Piecing

8" or 16" Block W
make 4

Block W Piecing

16" or 32" Unit 3
make 2

Unit 3 Piecing

16" or 32" Unit 4
make 2

Unit 4 Piecing

32" or 64" Block X
make 1

Block X Piecing

For either quilt size, make 8 each of units 1 and 2. Turning the blocks as shown, join each unit 1 to a unit 2 to make 8 half blocks. Join 2 halves to make a W block. Make 4 W's. Use these W's to make 2 each of units 3 and 4. Join each unit 3 to a unit 4 to make 2 X half blocks. Join halves to complete 1 X block.

SPARKLER PIECED BORDERS FOR 2 SIZES & QUILT CONSTRUCTION: WALL SIZE

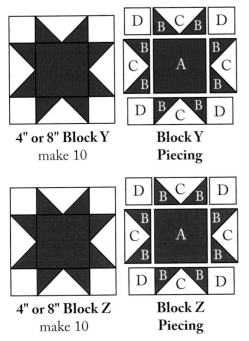

4" or 8" Block Y
make 10

Block Y Piecing

4" or 8" Block Z
make 10

Block Z Piecing

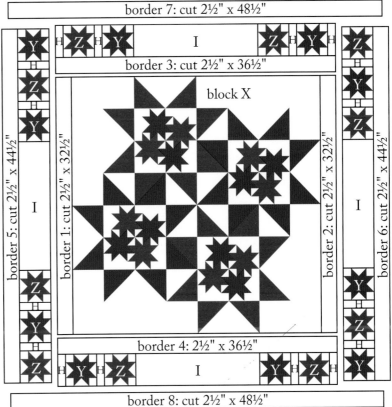

Whole Quilt Construction: Wall Size

See the border block diagrams, above. If you are making the wall quilt, make ten 4" Y and ten 4" Z blocks. If you are making the queen quilt, make ten 8" Y's and ten 8" Z's.

Sew the 2 shortest cream borders to the left and right sides of the X block, as shown above right or on page 26.

For this color variation, simply replace red with medium blue in the diagrams, yardage, and cutting lists.

See the quilt diagram for your quilt size, above or on the next page. Make the top pieced border from H-Z-H-Y-I-Z-H-Y-H. Sew a cream border of the shortest length that remains to the bottom of the top pieced border. Make the bottom pieced border exactly the same. Attach these to the top and bottom of the quilt, with the plain border touching the X block for both of these borders.

Make the left side border from Y-H-Z-H-Y-I-Z-H-Y-H-Z (from the top down). Attach the next-to-the-longest plain border to the left side of the left border, making sure you have oriented the border with the blue star at the top as shown. Repeat exactly for the right border, but turn it around so the plain border is on the right and the red star is at the top. Stitch the side borders to the quilt, with the cream strips on the outside edges.

Attach the remaining cream borders to the top and bottom of the quilt to complete the quilt top.

Quilt as desired and bind to finish.

25

QUEEN QUILT SPECIFICATIONS

Quilt Size: 96" x 96"
Block Size: 16" W blocks, 64" X block,
8" Y & Z blocks
Star Sizes: 8" and 32"
Requires: 8 unit 1, 8 unit 2, 2 unit 3,
2 unit 4, 4 W, 1 X, 10 Y, 10 Z

YARDAGE & CUTTING

1½ yards or 7 fat qtrs. ea. of Navy & Red:
(from each color cut the following)
16 E ◺ half-square triangles cut from
8 squares cut 8⅞"
18 A ☐ squares cut 4½"
144 B ◺ half-square triangles cut from
72 squares cut 2⅞"

7¾ yards White or Cream:
2 borders* cut 4½" x 96½"
2 borders* cut 4½" x 88½"
2 borders* cut 4½" x 72½"

White or Cream: *continued*
2 borders* cut 4½" x 64½"
8 I ☐ rectangles* cut 8½" x 32½"
8 F ⊠ quarter-square triangles cut from
2 squares cut 17¼"
8 E ◺ half-square triangles cut from
4 squares cut 8⅞"
4 G ☐ squares cut 8½"
32 H ☐ rectangles* cut 2½" x 8½"
112 C ⊠ quarter-square triangles cut
from 28 squares cut 5¼"
32 B ◺ half-square triangles cut from 16
squares cut 2⅞"
96 D ☐ squares cut 2½"

9¼ yards 44"-Wide Backing Fabric:
3 panels cut 35¼" x 104½"

¾ yard Binding Fabric:
2" x 394"

Rotary cut H and I rectangles and borders with the long edges on the lengthwise grain of the fabric.

Yardage and cutting for navy and red are identical. Buy 1½ yards of navy and 1½ yards of red. Cut the listed patches from each of the two colors.

Note that the queen-size quilt uses the same patch letters, diagrams, and instructions as the wall quilt. The patch dimensions and border lengths differ. Use the specifications, yardage and cutting above and the whole quilt diagram at right for the queen quilt. Use the quantities and block diagrams on page 24 and the left side of page 25 for both quilt sizes.

Be sure to read the text below the cutting charts on page 23, as well as all text on pages 24-25, as it applies to both sizes of the quilt.

Whole Quilt Construction: Queen Size

STARLIGHT MEDALLION

Starlight Medallion, 96" x 96", pieced by Sherry McConnell, Stephanie Crabtree, Alyce Taylor, and Cathy Goins; quilted by Linda Lupton, all of The Quilting Collective. The strong geometry of a medallion quilt pairs perfectly with a high-contrast two-color scheme here.

The border of a quilt that I designed in 2014 for Quilter's Newsletter's *45th anniversary provided the starting point for this 2020 design. I devised an interior border in reverse colors next. Finally, I added the Rising Star center blocks. The two block colorings echo the*

reversal of colors in the inner and outer borders. The small stars in the Rising Stars match those from the borders.

Make this quilt from just two solids or two prints for a bold, graphic look. Alternatively, opt for scraps for a more nuanced appearance and more opportunity to express your personality with a range of fabric choices.

A patriotic variation of Starlight Medallion is shown on page 21. That version is not a direct substitution. You can use the charts on page 17 to look up changes to the yardage figures.

QUILT SPECIFICATIONS

Quilt Size: 96" x 96"
Block Size: 12" U and V, 8" W and Y, 6" x 8" X and Z
Star Sizes: 6", 8" and 12"
Requires: 21 star 1, 28 star 2, 5 U, 4 V, 16 W, 16 X, 24 Y, 24 Z

YARDAGE & CUTTING

6½ yards or 26 fat quarters Red:
2 borders* cut 2½" x 96½"
2 borders* cut 2½" x 92½"
2 borders* cut 2½" x 76½"
2 borders* cut 2½" x 72½"
20 F ⊠ quarter-square triangles cut from 5 squares cut 7¼"
48 G ▭ rectangles* cut 1½" x 6½"
96 J ⊠ quarter-square triangles cut from 24 squares cut 5¼"
16 H ☐ squares cut 4½"
112 C ⊠ quarter-square triangles cut from 28 squares cut 4¼"
32 E ◺ half-square triangles cut from 16 squares cut 3⅞"
41 A ☐ squares cut 3½"
128 I ◺ half-square triangles cut from 64 squares cut 2⅞"
96 K ☐ squares cut 2½"
168 B ◺ half-square triangles cut from 84 squares cut 2⅜"
112 D ☐ squares cut 2"

YARDAGE & CUTTING, *continued*

6¼ yards or 25 fat quarters Cream:
2 borders* cut 4½" x 72½"
2 borders* cut 4½" x 64½"
2 borders* cut 6½" x 48½"
2 borders* cut 6½" x 36½"
16 F ⊠ quarter-square triangles cut from 4 squares cut 7¼"
32 G ▭ rectangles* cut 1½" x 6½"
64 J ⊠ quarter-square triangles cut from 16 squares cut 5¼"
24 H ☐ squares cut 4½"
84 C ⊠ quarter-square triangles cut from 21 squares cut 4¼"
40 E ◺ half-square triangles cut from 20 squares cut 3⅞"
44 A ☐ squares cut 3½"
192 I ◺ half-square triangles cut from 96 squares cut 2⅞"
64 K ☐ squares cut 2½"
224 B ◺ half-square triangles cut from 112 squares cut 2⅜"
84 D ☐ squares cut 2"

9¼ yards 44"-Wide Backing Fabric:
3 panels cut 35¼" x 104½"

¾ yard Binding Fabric:
2" x 394"

Rotary cut G rectangles and borders with the long edges on the lengthwise grain of the fabric.

If you use fat quarters, you can piece the borders from lengthwise strips cut about 18" x 2½"/4½"/6½".

Be sure to read the material at the front of the book that explains my method, identifies exactly what I include in my dimensions and yardage figures, teaches you how to get the most out of the diagrams, and details how to rotary cut and piece the Rising Star and Evening Star blocks.

Rotary cut the longest borders first, cutting parallel to the selvage. Then cut the shorter borders and the largest patches. They are listed in size order. Cut smaller patches from the leftovers. Cut rectangles with the long edge parallel to the selvage. You need not cut everything before you start sewing. You can cut a little and sew a little, if you like. If you plan to do that, start by cutting off a length sufficient for the borders and set it aside. Then use the remainder to cut the patches you intend to sew first.

If you wish, eliminate dogears by trimming the points of the B, C, E, F, I, and J triangles. Use the A trim of my Point Trimmer for B, E, and I triangles and the B trim for C, F, and J triangles. If you prefer, download charts and instructions for using a regular ruler to trim points by going to the RWB Extras page at

judymartin.com

STARLIGHT MEDALLION BLOCKS

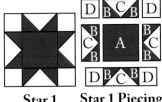

Star 1 **Star 1 Piecing**
make 21

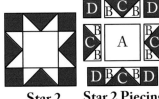

Star 2 **Star 2 Piecing**
make 28

Block U
make 5

Block U Piecing

Block V
make 4

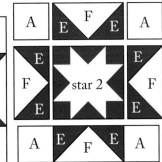

Block V Piecing

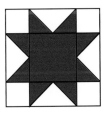

Block W
make 16

Block W Piecing

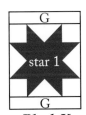

**Block X
& Piecing**
make 16

Block Y
make 24

Block Y Piecing

**Block Z
& Piecing**
make 24

See the diagrams above. Make 21 star 1's and 28 star 2's. (If you need step-by-step directions for cutting and piecing the Evening Stars and Rising Stars, see pages 12–13.)

Use the star 1's to make 5 U blocks for the quilt center and 16 X blocks for the inner borders.

Use the star 2's to make 4 V blocks for the quilt center and 24 Z blocks for the outer borders.

Also make 16 W blocks for the inner borders and 24 Y blocks for the outer borders.

For this navy-and-cream version of Starlight Medallion, substitute cream for red and navy for cream in all diagrams, cutting lists and yardage figures.

STARLIGHT MEDALLION QUILT CONSTRUCTION

Starlight Medallion Whole Quilt Construction

Assemble the quilt from blocks and plain borders as shown above. Start by joining U and V blocks alternately, three per vertical column. Stitch the columns together to make the quilt center. Add the 36½" cream borders to the quilt's right and left sides.

Make two pieced borders, each having 4 X blocks alternated with 3 W blocks. Stitch a 48½" cream border to one edge of each. Attach these to the top and bottom of the quilt, turning them so the cream borders touch the quilt center.

Next, make the inner right and left pieced borders, joining 5 W blocks alternately with 4 X blocks. Stitch a 64½" cream border to one edge of each.

Attach these to the quilt's right and left sides, with the plain borders on the outside edge. Add the 72½" cream borders to the quilt's top and bottom, followed by the 72½" red borders on the right and left.

Make two pieced borders having 6 Z blocks alternated with 5 Y blocks. Add a 76½" red border to one edge of each. Attach these to the top and bottom.

Make two side borders having 7 Y blocks alternated with 6 Z's. Stitch a 92½" red border to each. Sew these to the right and left sides of the quilt, with the plain borders on the outside. Add 96½" red borders to the top and bottom to complete the quilt top. Quilt as desired and bind to finish.

30

AMERICAN HERO

American Hero, 56" x 72", pieced by Marilyn Deppe and quilted by Carol Westercamp. This quilt packs a powerful punch. How many quilts of this size and scale require just 23 blocks? And how many quilts made from the most basic of stars look as fresh and new as American Hero, with its bold band of stars?

I designed this quilt in 2014, though it is published here for the first time. I often design in series, and this one followed my Anniversary Stars, the same quilt that inspired Starlight Medallion on page 27. Here, my goal was to minimize the piecing by limiting it to a diagonal swath across the quilt. In this case, as with many of my quilts, I followed the rule, "Laziness is the mother of invention." The flair of the quilt comes from the same diagonal swath that makes it easy. My lazy mantra also inspired my combination of two star sizes. This element adds interest while also eliminating fussy joints. This simple, stylish quilt is appropriate for a Quilt of Valor®.

A blue-and-white version of American Hero is on page 19. It replaces red with medium blue.

QUILT SPECIFICATIONS

Quilt Size: 56" x 72"
Block Size: 8"
Star Sizes: 6" and 8"
Requires: 7 star 1, 14 X, 7 Y, 2 Z blocks

YARDAGE & CUTTING

⅞ yard or 4 or more fat quarters Blue:

12 M ◨ half-square triangles cut from
  6 squares cut 8⅞"

2 G ☐ squares cut 4½"

7 A ☐ squares cut 3½"

16 H ◨ half-square triangles cut from
  8 squares cut 2⅞"

56 B ◨ half-square triangles cut from
  28 squares cut 2⅜"

1⅞ yards or 8 or more fat quarters Red:

2 L ◺ half trapezoids* cut from
  2 rectangles** cut 8½" x 40⅞"

2 Lr ◿ half trapezoids* cut from
  2 rectangles** cut 8½" x 40⅞"

14 G ☐ squares cut 4½"

112 H ◨ half-square triangles cut from
  56 squares cut 2⅞"

2⅜ yards White or Cream:

2 K ◨ half-square triangles cut from
  1 square cut 32⅞"***

14 F ▭ rectangles** cut 1½" x 8½"

14 E ▭ rectangles** cut 1½" x 6½"

64 I ⊠ quarter-square triangles cut from
  16 squares cut 5¼"

28 C ⊠ quarter-square triangles cut from
  7 squares cut 4¼"

64 J ☐ squares cut 2½"

28 D ☐ squares cut 2"

4¾ yards 44"-Wide Backing Fabric:
2 panels cut 32½" x 80½"

½ yard Binding Fabric:
2" x 266"

Cut L and Lr half trapezoids as shown at right.

**Rotary cut rectangles for E, F, L and Lr with the long edges on the lengthwise grain of the fabric.*

***In order to rotary cut the large K triangles, you will need to place two large rulers side by side. Note whether or not the rulers have overall dimensions in whole inches or half inches, as you will need to add one ruler's dimension to the other in order to cut a square 32⅞".*

If you have just one ruler, you will need to mark a chalk line or pencil line along the ruler's edge, then slide the ruler over a little and extend the line to the needed length. Mark off the entire square, double-check your measurements, then lay your ruler along the line to rotary cut the square. Carefully fold the square in half diagonally, and crease the fold. Open the fold and align your ruler with the crease to rotary cut the square into two triangles, sliding the ruler along the crease as needed to complete the cut.

Be sure to read the material at the front of the book that explains my method, identifies exactly what I include in my dimensions and yardage figures, teaches you how to get the most out of the diagrams, and details how to rotary cut and piece the Evening Star blocks.

Rotary cut the K, L, Lr, and M patches before you cut the smaller patches from the same color. The patches are listed in size order, from largest to smallest. Cut smaller patches from the leftovers. Cut rectangles with the long edge parallel to the selvage.

You need not cut everything before you start sewing. You can cut a little and sew a little, if you like.

If you wish, you can eliminate dogears by trimming the points of the B, C, H, I, K, L, Lr, and M patches. Use my Point Trimmer tool or download charts and instructions for using your regular ruler to trim points by going to the RWB Extras page at judymartin.com

For the B, H, K, and M triangles and L and Lr half trapezoids, use the A trim of my tool or the downloaded A chart; for the C and I triangles, use the B trim of my tool or the downloaded B chart.

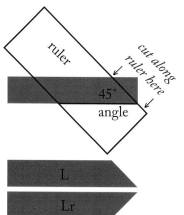

Cut rectangles for L and Lr from folded fabric. Align the 45-degree angle of your ruler with the corner of the rectangle stack, as shown. Cut off a waste triangle to make L and Lr patches.

AMERICAN HERO BLOCKS & QUILT CONSTRUCTION

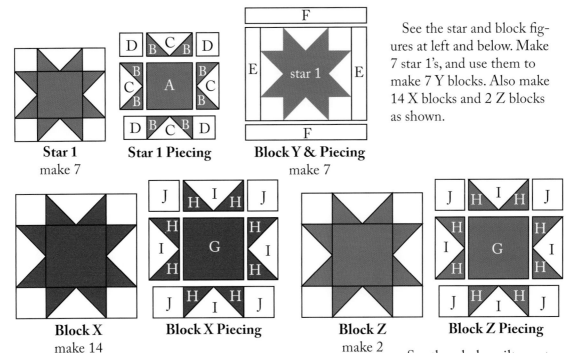

Star 1
make 7

Star 1 Piecing

Block Y & Piecing
make 7

See the star and block figures at left and below. Make 7 star 1's, and use them to make 7 Y blocks. Also make 14 X blocks and 2 Z blocks as shown.

Block X
make 14

Block X Piecing

Block Z
make 2

Block Z Piecing

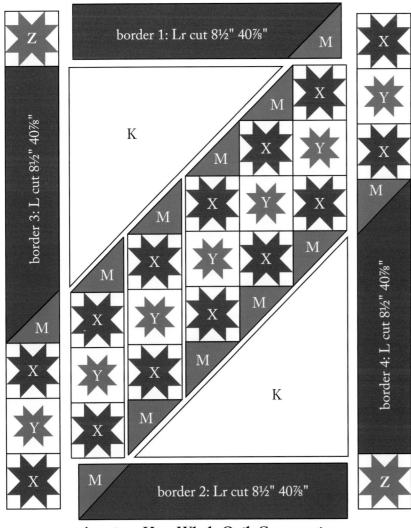

American Hero Whole Quilt Construction

See the whole quilt construction diagram at left. Join X-Y-X blocks in a vertical column. Repeat to make 7 columns like this. Add an M triangle to each end of the three center columns, as shown. Add an M to just one end of the right and left columns of the quilt center. Join these 5 columns for the quilt center. Attach a cream K triangle to the top left and bottom right to complete a rectangle.

See the L and Lr cutting directions on the previous page. Cut off one end of each L rectangle at a 45-degree angle to make 2 L and 2 Lr (reversed) half trapezoids.

Stitch an M triangle to the angled end of each red L and Lr. Stitch one Lr-M border to the top of the rectangular center and the other Lr-M border to the bottom, turning them as shown.

Make the side borders, attaching one of the remaining X-Y-X columns to the M end of an L-M border. Stitch a Z block to the opposite end to complete a side border. Repeat for the other side. Sew these to the right and left of the quilt, turning them as shown.

Quilt and bind to finish.

STARS OVER THE STATES

Stars Over the States, 95" x 95", pieced by Tammie Klein and Neil Thompson and quilted by John Kerstein of 2 Guyz Quilting. This quilt, with its 140 stars, was not designed to be made overnight. If you are willing to put in the time and effort, this pattern will reward you with an heirloom-quality quilt that you can be proud of.

I designed Stars Over the States on July 4, 2010. It originally had my Staggered Star border from a quilt I designed in 1994. I changed the border slightly for this quilt, as I wanted it to echo the arrangement of stars in the quilt center. I followed the path of the stars when I changed background colors in the blocks and borders.

This design is perfect for a high-contrast color scheme such as this. To make it in two colors, simply add together the yardages and patch cutting for the red and blue. You can make the 2-color version with dark stars on a light background if you prefer. Be sure to see the four color variations on page 20.

STARS OVER THE STATES INSTRUCTIONS

QUILT SPECIFICATIONS

Quilt Size: 95" x 95"

Block Size: 20" W blocks, 5" x 10" X & Y border blocks, 10" Z corner blocks

Star Size: 5"

Requires: 68 star 1, 32 star 2, 36 star 3, 18 u. 1, 36 u. 2, 9 W, 32 X, 28 Y, 4 Z

YARDAGE & CUTTING

4⅞ yards Navy Blue:

4 ☐ long sashes* cut 1¾" x 65½"

12 ☐ short sashes* cut 1¾" x 20½"

36 F ☐ rectangles* cut 3" x 8"

4 K ☐ squares cut 5½"

32 I ☐ rectangles* cut 4¼" x 5½"

36 E ☐ rectangles* cut 3" x 5½"

36 H ☐ rectangles* cut 1¾" x 5½"

320 C ☒ quarter-square triangles cut from 80 squares cut 3¾"

316 D ☐ squares cut 1¾"

4½ yards Red:

2 borders* cut 5½" x 75½"

2 borders* cut 5½" x 65½"

9 G ☐ rectangles* cut 5½" x 10½"

28 I ☐ rectangles* cut 4¼" x 5½"

18 E ☐ rectangles* cut 3" x 5½"

32 H ☐ rectangles* cut 1¾" x 5½"

4 J ☐ squares cut 4¼"

240 C ☒ quarter-square triangles cut from 60 squares cut 3¾"

240 D ☐ squares cut 1¾"

3¼ yards or 13 fat qtrs. White or Cream:

140 A ☐ squares cut 3"

1120 B ◩ half-square triangles cut from 560 squares cut 2⅛"

9⅛ yards 44"-Wide Backing Fabric:

3 panels cut 35" x 103½"

or 3⅛ yards 108"-Wide Backing Fabric:

1 panel cut 103½" x 103½"

¾ yard Binding Fabric:

2" x 390"

Rotary cut E, F, G, H, and I rectangles, short and long sashes, and borders with the long edges on the lengthwise grain of the fabric.

Be sure to read the material at the front of the book that explains my method, identifies exactly what I include in my dimensions and yardage figures, teaches you how to get the most out of the diagrams, and details how to rotary cut and piece the Evening Star blocks.

Rotary cut the borders and larger patches before you cut the smaller patches from the same color. The patches are listed in size order, from largest to smallest. Cut smaller patches from the leftovers. Cut rectangles with the long edge parallel to the selvage.

You need not cut everything before you start sewing. You can cut a little and sew a little, if you like. If you plan to do that, be sure to reserve a sufficient length fabric for the sashes and borders.

If you wish, eliminate dogears by trimming the points of the B and C triangles. Use the A trim of my Point Trimmer for B triangles and B trim for C triangles. If you prefer, download charts and instructions for using a regular ruler to trim points by going to the RWB Extras page at *judymartin.com*

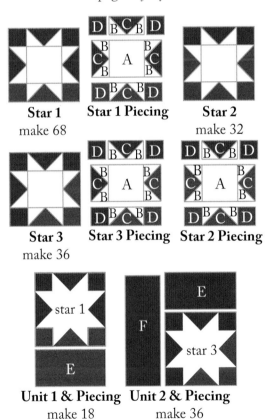

Star 1 make 68   **Star 1 Piecing**   **Star 2** make 32

Star 3 make 36   **Star 3 Piecing**   **Star 2 Piecing**

Unit 1 & Piecing make 18   **Unit 2 & Piecing** make 36

Make stars 1, 2, and 3 in the quantities listed above. Use the star 1's to make unit 1's, above, and blocks W, Y, and Z on the next page. Use star 2's to make X blocks, as shown on the next page. Use star 3's to make unit 2's, above. Units 1 and 2, shown above, are used to make W blocks.

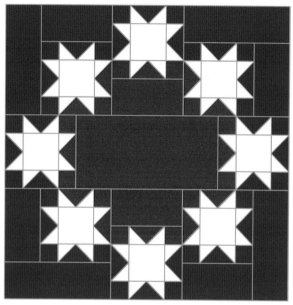

Block W
make 9

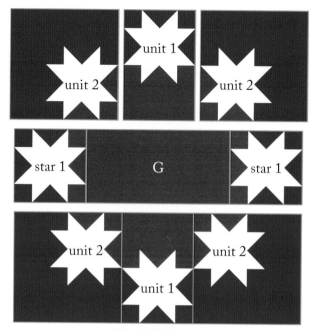

Block W Piecing

After making stars 1, 2, and 3 and units 1 and 2, as shown on the previous page, you should have patches left over for the partial stars in the Z corner blocks. Assemble star 1's, red G's, unit 1's, and unit 2's to make 9 W blocks as shown above. Be careful to turn the blocks as shown, with the red on the inside and blue on the outside of the block.

After you make the W blocks, you will have 32 star 1's and all of the star 2's left over for making the X, Y, and Z border blocks, shown below.

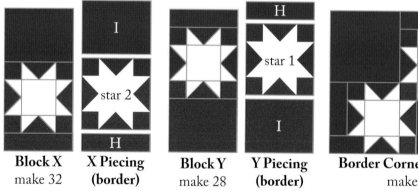

Block X
make 32

X Piecing (border)

Block Y
make 28

Y Piecing (border)

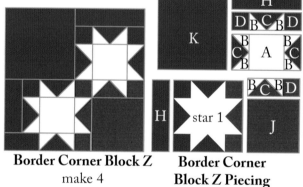

Border Corner Block Z
make 4

Border Corner Block Z Piecing

Use the star 2's to make 32 border block X's as shown above. Use 28 of the remaining star 1's to make 28 border block Y's. The 4 remaining star 1's are used in the 4 Z blocks. Make Z in 2 halves, with the block divided horizontally. Note that the top star in the Z block has parts in both halves of the block.

STARS OVER THE STATES QUILT CONSTRUCTION

Stars Over the States Whole Quilt Construction

Referring to the diagram above, make a block row from 4 short blue sashes alternated with 3 W blocks. Make three block rows like this. Join 3 block rows alternately with 2 long blue sashes.

Join 7 Y's alternately with 6 X's for the top pieced border. Sew a long blue 65½" sash to a 65½" red border. Sew the red edge of this unit to the red side of the top pieced border. Repeat to make an identical bottom border. Sew one of these to the top of the quilt and the other to the bottom, turning the borders with the plain blue strip on the inside.

For a side border, sew 8 X blocks alternately with 7 Y blocks, turning the blocks as shown above. Add a Z corner block to each end, turning the Z blocks to match the diagram. Stitch the red end of an X block to each short end of a 75½" plain red border. Stitch this to the red edge of the side border to complete the side border unit. Repeat to make an identical border unit for the opposite side. Stitch these two border units to the right and left sides of the quilt, turning them as shown, to complete the quilt top.

Quilt as desired and bind to finish.

SHAKESPEARE IN THE PARK
QUEEN SIZE

Shakespeare in the Park, 96⅜" x 96⅜", pieced by me in 2020 and quilted by Debbi Treusch. This quilt is the most popular pattern I have ever published.

I designed this quilt for The Creative Pattern Book in 2000. The pattern appeared in Quilter's Newsletter in 2001. I also published slight variations of this quilt as *Virginia Stars Sampler* in Knockout Blocks & Sampler Quilts *in 2004 and as* Jewel of the Prairie *in* Love

of Quilting in 2005. In spite of all these opportunities, I didn't get the chance to make the quilt until now.

The quilt's name is a reference to my high school days in San Diego, where I spent many weekends ushering at the Old Globe Theater in Balboa Park in return for free admission to the Shakespeare plays.

A patriotic version is shown on page 21. The charts on page 17 will help you adjust the yardage figures for it.

QUEEN QUILT SPECIFICATIONS

Quilt Size: 96⅜" x 96⅜"
Block Size: 12"
Star Sizes: 6" and 12"
Requires: 28 star 1, 28 star 2, 8 X, 8 Y,
25 Z, 2 unit 1, 2 unit 2, 4 unit 3,
4 unit 4, 4 unit 5, 4 unit 6

YARDAGE & CUTTING

7⅜ yards or 30 fat quarters Red:
2 borders* cut 2" x 96⅞"
2 borders* cut 2" x 93⅞"
44 K ⊠ quarter-square triangles cut from
11 squares cut 9¾"

5⅞ yards or 24 fat quarters Cream:
and remaining Red:
(from each color cut the following)
32 F ⊠ quarter-square triangles cut from
8 squares cut 7¼"
50 I ◩ half-square triangles cut from
25 squares cut 6⅞"
8 J ☐ squares cut 6½"
50 H ◩ half-square triangles cut from
25 squares cut 5⅛"
112 C ⊠ quarter-square triangles cut
from 28 squares cut 4¼"
114 E ◩ half-square triangles cut from
57 squares cut 3⅞"
60 A ☐ squares cut 3½"
50 G ◩ half-square triangles cut from
25 squares cut 3"
224 B ◩ half-square triangles cut from
112 squares cut 2⅜"
162 D ☐ squares cut 2"

9¼ yards 44"-Wide Backing Fabric:
3 panels cut 35⅜" x 104⅞"

¾ yard Binding Fabric:
2" x 396"

Rotary cut borders with the long edges on the lengthwise grain of the fabric.

Be sure to read the material at the front of the book that explains my method, identifies exactly what I include in my dimensions and yardage figures, teaches you how to get the most out of the diagrams, and details how to rotary cut and piece the Rising Star and Evening Star blocks.

Rotary cut the longest borders first, cutting parallel to the selvage. Then cut the shorter borders and the largest patches. They are listed in size order. Cut smaller patches from the leftovers.

If you are using scraps or fat quarters, you can piece the borders from 2" x 17" or 2" x 18" strips of numerous similarly colored fat quarters.

You need not cut everything before you start sewing. You can cut a little and sew a little, if you like. If you plan to do that, start by cutting off a length sufficient for the borders and set it aside. Then use the remainder to cut the patches you intend to sew first.

I strongly recommend trimming the points on the E, G, H, I, and K triangles in order to help you align the patches for piecing. Use the C trim on my Point Trimmer tool, or download the file and instructions for making your own C point trimming guide by going to the RWB Extras page at

judymartin.com

If you wish, you can eliminate dogears by also trimming the points of the B, C, and F triangles. For B triangles, use the A trim of my tool or your downloaded file; for C and F triangles, use the B trim. Download charts and instructions for using your regular ruler to trim points at the web address above.

For this option, substitute navy for cream and white for red in the yardage, cutting lists, and diagrams.

Star 1
make 28

Star 1 Piecing

Star 2
make 28

Star 2 Piecing

Block X
make 8

Block X Piecing

Block Y
make 8

Block Y Piecing

Block Z
make 25

Block Z Patches

Block Z Piecing Sequence

Note that patches C & G are the same size. Patches F & H are also the same size. I distinguish them because the grain and cutting method differ.

Referring to the diagrams above, make 28 each of stars 1 and 2. Use 8 star 1's to make X blocks. Use 8 star 2's to make Y blocks. Reserve the remaining stars 1 and 2 for use in the border units.

When cutting triangles for the Z blocks, use my Point Trimmer tool's C trim to trim the points. This will help you align the ends of each triangle with the ends of the block to which you stitch it. Pin both ends of the seams to avoid stretching bias edges. Make 25 Z blocks, following the patches diagram to identify patch letters and referring to the piecing sequence figure to determine the sewing order.

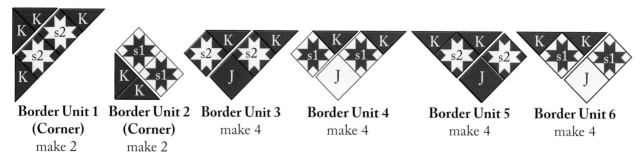

Border Unit 1 (Corner)
make 2

Border Unit 2 (Corner)
make 2

Border Unit 3
make 4

Border Unit 4
make 4

Border Unit 5
make 4

Border Unit 6
make 4

Referring to the diagrams above, use the remaining stars 1 and 2 to make border units in the listed quantities. Make each in 2 diagonal rows, sewing the seam between exploded parts last.

Shakespeare in the Park Whole Quilt Construction: Queen

Study the whole quilt diagram above. You will be making diagonal rows of varying lengths with border units on the ends. The longer rows alternate Z and Y blocks or Z and X blocks. Every Z within a row is oriented the same, but Z's in Y rows are turned differently from Z's in X rows.

Each successive row is 2 blocks or units longer than the last until you pass the sixth row. If you start in the upper left corner of the quilt, row 1 has only a unit 1. Row 2 has u6/Z/u4. Row 3 consists of u5/Z/Y/Z/u3. Row 4 has u6/Z/X/Z/X/Z/u4. Row 5 has u5/Z/Y/Z/Y/Z/Y/Z/u3. Row 6 has u2/Z/X/Z/X/Z/X/Z/X/Z/u2. The 5 rows beyond the center row are exactly like the first 5 rows. Make rows as shown.

Join rows 1–5. Make an identical segment by joining rows 7–11. Add row six to one segment. Stitch the remaining segment to the other side of row 6.

Add the 93⅞"-long red borders to opposite sides of the quilt. Add the 96⅞"-long borders to the top and bottom to complete the quilt top.

41

SHAKESPEARE IN THE PARK
TWIN SIZE

Shakespeare in the Park, 76⅜" x 93⅜", pieced by Margy Sieck and quilted by Jean Nolte. This quilt was made in 2000 for The Creative Pattern Book. *The quilt's high-contrast 2-color scheme, scrap nuances, swirling movement, and star blocks make it a perennial favorite.*

My design busted norms in 2000 by combining five types, colors, and sizes of blocks in a single quilt. I have frequently employed more than two types and sizes of blocks in more recent work, including this book, which has a half-dozen examples.

TWIN QUILT SPECIFICATIONS

Quilt Size: 76⅜" x 93⅜"
Block Size: 12"
Star Sizes: 6" and 12"
Requires: 24 star 1, 24 star 2, 6 X, 6 Y, 20 Z, 1 unit 1, 1 unit 2, 3 unit 3, 3 unit 4, 4 unit 5, 4 unit 6, 1 unit 7, 1 unit 8

YARDAGE & CUTTING

1 yard or 4 or more fat qtrs. Med. Blue:
40 K ⊠ quarter-square triangles cut from 10 squares cut 9¾"

4¾ yards each of Dk. Blue and Cream or 19 fat quarters of each: (from each color cut the following)
24 F ⊠ quarter-square triangles cut from 6 squares cut 7¼"
40 I ◩ half-square triangles cut from 20 squares cut 6⅞"
7 J ☐ squares cut 6½"
40 H ◩ half-square triangles cut from 20 squares cut 5⅛"
96 C ⊠ quarter-square triangles cut from 24 squares cut 4¼"
88 E ◩ half-square triangles cut from 44 squares cut 3⅞"
48 A ☐ squares cut 3½"
40 G ◩ half-square triangles cut from 20 squares cut 3"
192 B ◩ half-square triangles cut from 96 squares cut 2⅜"
136 D ☐ squares cut 2"

7½ yards 44"-Wide Backing Fabric:
3 panels cut 34⅜" x 84⅞"

¾ yard Binding Fabric:
2" x 350"

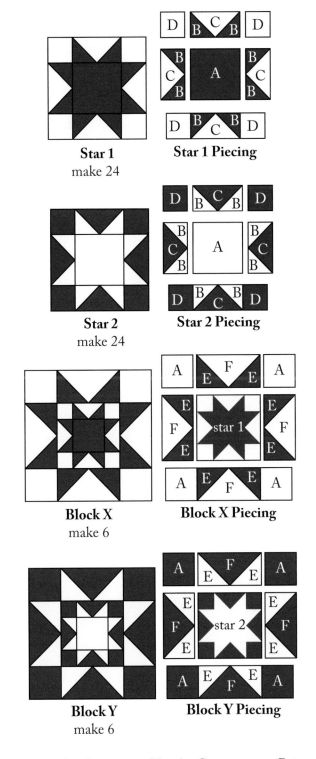

Star 1
make 24

Star 1 Piecing

Star 2
make 24

Star 2 Piecing

Block X
make 6

Block X Piecing

Block Y
make 6

Block Y Piecing

Be sure to read the material at the front of the book that explains my method, identifies exactly what I include in my dimensions and yardage figures, and teaches you how to get the most out of the diagrams.

Rotary cut the largest patches first. Then cut the smaller patches from the leftovers. They are listed in size order, from largest to smallest.

I strongly recommend trimming the points on the E, G, H, I, and K triangles in order to help you align

the patches for piecing. Use the C trim on my Point Trimmer tool, or download instructions for making your own C point trimming guide by going to the RWB Extras page at judymartin.com

Eliminate dogears by also trimming points of the B, C, and F triangles. For B triangles, use the A trim of my tool or your downloaded file; for C and F, use the B trim. Download instructions for using your regular ruler to trim points at my website, above.

SHAKESPEARE IN THE PARK TWIN BLOCKS & UNITS

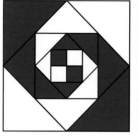

Block Z
make 20

Block Z Patches

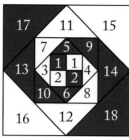

**Block Z Piecing
Sequence**

Note that patches C & G are the same size. Patches F & H are also the same size. I distinguish them because the grain and cutting method differ.

I strongly recommend trimming the points on the E, G, H, and I triangles of the Z block to help you align patches for stitching. See the note at the bottom of the previous page.

Referring to the diagrams on the previous page, make 24 each of stars 1 and 2. Use 6 star 1's to make X blocks. Use 6 star 2's to make Y blocks. Reserve the remaining stars 1 and 2 for use later in the border units.

See the diagrams above. When cutting triangles for the Z blocks, trim points using my Point

Trimmer or download instructions to make one, as listed on page 43. This will help you align the ends of each triangle with the ends of the block to which you stitch it. Pin both ends of the seams to avoid stretching bias edges. Make 20 Z blocks, following the diagram to identify patch letters and referring to the piecing sequence to determine the sewing order.

**Border Unit 1
(Corner)**
make 1

**Border Unit 2
(Corner)**
make 1

Border Unit 3
make 3

Border Unit 4
make 3

Border Unit 5
make 4

Border Unit 6
make 4

**Border Unit 7
(Corner)**
make 1

**Border Unit 8
(Corner)**
make 1

Referring to the diagrams above, use the remaining stars 1 and 2 to make border units in the listed quantities. Make each in 2 diagonal rows, sewing the seam between exploded parts last.

This version of the twin Shakespeare in the Park makes straightforward substitutions. Simply substitute navy for medium blue and red for dark blue in the yardage, cutting lists, and diagrams.

SHAKESPEARE IN THE PARK TWIN QUILT CONSTRUCTION

Shakespeare in the Park Whole Quilt Construction: Twin

Study the whole quilt diagram above. You will be making diagonal rows of varying lengths with border units on the ends. Rows 3, 5, and 7 alternate Z and Y blocks; rows 4, 6, and 8 alternate Z and X blocks. Every Z within a row is oriented the same, but Z's in Y rows are turned differently from Z's in X rows.

If you start in the upper left corner of the quilt, row 1 has only unit 1. Row 2 has u5/Z/u4. Row 3 has u6/Z/Y/Z/u3. Row 4 has u5/Z/X/Z/X/Z/u4.

Row 5 has u6/Z/Y/Z/Y/Z/Y/Z/u7. Row 6 has u2/Z/X/Z/X/Z/X/Z/u5. Each successive row is 2 blocks or units longer than the last until you pass the row 5. After row 6, each successive row is 2 blocks or units shorter. Row 7 has u3/Z/Y/Z/Y/Z/u6. Row 8 has u4/Z/X/Z/u5. Row 9 has u3/Z/u6. Row 10 has only unit 8. Join blocks and units to make rows.

Join rows 1–10 in numerical order, as shown above. Quilt as desired and bind to finish.

45

THE RED, WHITE & BLUE: QUEEN

The Red, White & Blue, 94" x 94", pieced by Mary Bird and quilted by Vicki Bales. Stars and stripes cast their shadows on a cream background in this fresh quilt.

I designed this star in 2005 as the center of a Log Cabin block for Judy Martin's Log Cabin Quilt Book. I subtracted the logs, added the striped border, and recolored it all for this version.

Mary made The Red, White & Blue from a handful of red and navy prints against a single background fabric.

Her prints read as mostly solid. You could use four solids for a similar look overall. However, solids would appear more starkly graphic when viewed up close. For a different look, you could use a scrappy variety of red and blue prints. Even in a scrap quilt, I would recommend using a single background fabric and a single gray in order to achieve the most realistic shadow illusion.

I present the pattern here in two sizes: queen and throw. The throw size is Quilt of Valor® appropriate.

THE RED, WHITE & BLUE INSTRUCTIONS: TWO SIZES

QUEEN QUILT SPECIFICATIONS

Quilt Size: 94" x 94"
Block Size: 10" W & X blocks, 4" x 10" Y & Z border blocks
Star Size: 8"
Requires: 18 W, 22 X, 36 Y, 36 Z

YARDAGE & CUTTING

1⅛ yards or 5 or more fat qtrs. Navy:
22 A ☐ squares cut 4½"
176 B ◺ half-square triangles cut from 88 squares cut 2⅞"

2⅜ yards or 10 fat quarters Red:
72 F ☐ rectangles* cut 2½" x 8½"
18 A ☐ squares cut 4½"
144 B ◺ half-square triangles cut from 72 squares cut 2⅞"

2⅜ yards Gray:
72 H ☐ rectangles* cut 1½" x 8½"
80 C ⊠ quarter-square triangles cut from 20 squares cut 5¼"
160 B ◺ half-square triangles cut from 80 squares cut 2⅞"
40 D ☐ squares cut 2½"
72 G ☐ squares cut 1½"

5⅞ yards White or Cream:
1 border* cut 2½" x 94½"
1 border* cut 2½" x 92½"
2 borders* cut 6½" x 72½"
2 borders* cut 6½" x 60½"
72 J ☐ rectangles* cut 1½" x 10½"
160 C ⊠ quarter-square triangles cut from 40 squares cut 5¼"
80 E ☐ rectangles* cut 2½" x 4½"
72 I ☐ rectangles* cut 1½" x 3½"
160 D ☐ squares cut 2½"
144 G ☐ squares cut 1½"

9⅛ yards 44"-Wide Backing Fabric:
3 panels cut 34½" x 102½"

¾ yard Binding Fabric:
2" x 386"

THROW QUILT SPECIFICATIONS

Quilt Size: 66" x 78"
Block Size: 10" W & X blocks, 4" x 10" Y & Z border blocks
Star Size: 8"
Requires: 10 W, 14 X, 22 Y, 28 Z

YARDAGE & CUTTING

¾ yard or 3 or more fat qtrs. Navy Blue:
14 A ☐ squares cut 4½"
112 B ◺ half-square triangles cut from 56 squares cut 2⅞"

1⅝ yards or 7 or more fat quarters Red:
50 F ☐ rectangles* cut 2½" x 8½"
10 A ☐ squares cut 4½"
80 B ◺ half-square triangles cut from 40 squares cut 2⅞"

1½ yards Gray:
50 H ☐ rectangles* cut 1½" x 8½"
48 C ⊠ quarter-square triangles cut from 12 squares cut 5¼"
96 B ◺ half-square triangles cut from 48 squares cut 2⅞"
24 D ☐ squares cut 2½"
50 G ☐ squares cut 1½"

3⅜ yards White or Cream:
1 border* cut 2½" x 76½"
1 border* cut 2½" x 66½"
2 borders* cut 2½" x 50½"
2 borders* cut 3½" x 44½"
50 J ☐ rectangles* cut 1½" x 10½"
96 C ⊠ quarter-square triangles cut from 24 squares cut 5¼"
48 E ☐ rectangles* cut 2½" x 4½"
50 I ☐ rectangles* cut 1½" x 3½"
96 D ☐ squares cut 2½"
100 G ☐ squares cut 1½"

5⅛ yards 44"-Wide Backing Fabric:
2 panels cut 37½" x 86½"

½ yard Binding Fabric:
2" x 298"

Rotary cut E, F, H, I, and J rectangles and borders with the long edges on the lengthwise grain of the fabric.

Optional: Use the A trim on my Point Trimmer on B's; use B trim on C's. Or download a file to trim points by going to the RWB Extras page at judymartin.com

THE RED, WHITE & BLUE BLOCKS: TWO SIZES
Tips for a Successful Shadow Illusion

I suggest using a single fabric (not scraps) for the background. Use just one fabric for the shadows, as well. For realism, the fabric for the shadows should be a darker and duller shade of the background color, probably darker than your first inclination. If you use prints for the shadow and background, they should read as solids. The shadow fabric must also contrast with the reds and blues of the stars, so it should be a different value. Whether you are choosing fabric at the store or in your stash, you can judge contrasts as follows: Place the shadow fabric next to the star and background fabrics and snap a digital photo (preferably black and white). Alternatively, view them through a reducing glass or ruby beholder. Adjust your fabric selection as needed before you start cutting patches for the quilt.

Be sure to read the material at the front of the book that explains my method, identifies exactly what I include in my dimensions and yardage figures, teaches you how to get the most out of the diagrams, and details how to rotary cut and piece the Evening Star blocks.

Rotary cut the longest borders first, cutting parallel to the selvage. Then cut the shorter borders and the largest patches. They are listed in size order. Cut smaller patches from the leftovers.

You need not cut everything before you start sewing. You can cut a little and sew a little, if you like.

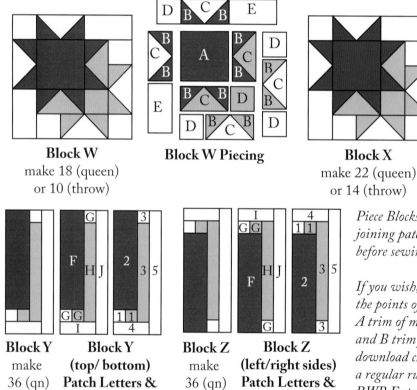

Block W
make 18 (queen)
or 10 (throw)

Block W Piecing

Block X
make 22 (queen)
or 14 (throw)

Block X Piecing

Block Y
make
36 (qn)
or 22 (th)

Block Y
(top/ bottom)
Patch Letters &
Piecing Order

Block Z
make
36 (qn)
or 28 (th)

Block Z
(left/right sides)
Patch Letters &
Piecing Order

Piece Blocks Y and Z in numerical order, joining patches having the same numbers before sewing them to the block.

If you wish, eliminate dogears by trimming the points of the B and C triangles. Use the A trim of my Point Trimmer for B triangles and B trim for C triangles. If you prefer, download charts and instructions for using a regular ruler to trim points by going to the RWB Extras page at judymartin.com

Referring to the diagrams above, make blocks W, X, Y, and Z in the quantities listed for your chosen quilt size. Reserve four X blocks for the border corners. The remaining X and W blocks are for the quilt center. The Y blocks are for the top and bottom borders. The Z blocks are for the side borders.

Queen: See the diagram at the top of page 49. Keep all blocks turned as shown, with the shadow at the bottom and right in all cases. Join 3 W and 3 X blocks alternately to make a row. Make rows 1 ("r1"), 3, and 5 of the quilt center with a red W block at the left end. Make rows 2, 4, and 6 with a blue X at the left. Join rows, alternating those starting with red and those starting with blue. Add a 60½" cream border to the left and right sides of the quilt, as shown.

Again, keeping all blocks turned as shown in the diagram at the top of page 49, join 18 Y blocks to *continued at the top of the next page*

THE RED, WHITE & BLUE QUILT: 2 SIZES

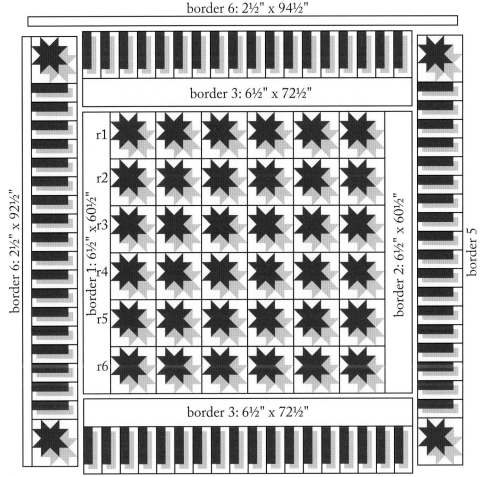

border 6: 2½" x 94½"

border 3: 6½" x 72½"

r1 r2 r3 r4 r5 r6

border 1: 6½" x 60½"

border 2: 6½" x 60½"

border 6: 2½" x 92½"

border 5

border 3: 6½" x 72½"

Whole Quilt Construction: Queen

continued from page 48 make the top border; repeat to make a bottom border. Add a 72½" cream border to the bottom edge of the top border and to the top edge of the bottom border. Add these to the quilt.

Join 18 Z blocks for the left border, adding an X block to each end. Repeat for the right border. Sew a 92½" cream border to the left side of the left border. Stitch the side borders to the quilt.

Add the 94½" cream border to the top of the quilt. Quilt and bind.

Queen: Use 18 Y each for top and bottom borders. Use 18 Z and 2 X each for sides.

Throw: Use 11 Y each for top and bottom borders. Use 14 Z and 2 X each for sides.

Throw: See the diagram at right. Keep all blocks turned as shown, with the shadow at the bottom and right in all cases. Join 2 W and 2 X blocks alternately to make a row. Make rows 1 (labeled "r1"), 3, and 5 of the quilt center with a red W block at the left end. Make rows 2 and 4 with a blue X block on the left. Join rows, alternating those starting with red and those starting with blue. Add a 50½" cream border to the left and right sides, as shown.

Keeping all blocks turned as shown, join 11 Y blocks to make the top border; repeat to make a bottom border. Add a 44½" cream border to the bottom edge of the top border and to the top edge of the bottom one. Stitch these to the quilt.

Join 14 Z blocks for the left border, adding an X block to each end. Repeat for the right border. Sew a 76½" cream border to the left side of the left border. Stitch the side borders to the quilt.

Add the 66½" cream border to the top of the quilt. Quilt as desired and bind to finish.

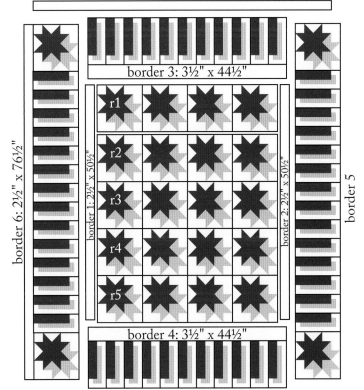

border 7: 2½" x 66½"

border 3: 3½" x 44½"

r1 r2 r3 r4 r5

border 6: 2½" x 76½"

border 1: 2½" x 50½"

border 2: 2½" x 50½"

border 5

border 4: 3½" x 44½"

Whole Quilt Construction: Throw

JULY FIREWORKS

July Fireworks, 96" x 96", was pieced by Chris Hulin and quilted by Carol Westercamp. Basic squares and triangles combine here to suggest the curves of a Double Wedding Ring.

When I designed this quilt in 2017, I did not anticipate the curved appearance, but when I saw it emerging, I tweaked the design to heighten the effect. The pieced *border echoes the curve of the quilt center and reinforces the illusion.*

I recommend a single fabric or tightly sorted scraps for the white. A solid or near solid will show off your quilting in the wide, plain borders.

Be sure to see the 2-color variation of July Fireworks on page 18.

QUILT SPECIFICATIONS

Quilt Size: 96" x 96"
Block Size: 12" T, 6" x 12" U, 3" x 6" V,
6" W, 7½" x 9" X, 6" x 7½" Y, 7½" Z
Star Size: 6"
Requires: 29 star 1, 48 unit 1, 20 unit 2,
24 unit 3, 9 T, 12 U, 8 V, 4 W, 20 X,
16 Y, 4 Z

YARDAGE & CUTTING

1½ yards or 6 or more fat quarters Red:
192 C ⊠ quarter-square triangles cut
from 48 squares cut 4¼"
16 A ☐ squares cut 3½"
128 B ◺ half-square triangles cut from
64 squares cut 2⅜"
40 D ☐ squares cut 2"

1¾ yds. or 7 or more fat quarters Navy:
80 C ⊠ quarter-square triangles cut from
20 squares cut 4¼"
29 A ☐ squares cut 3½"
232 B ◺ half-square triangles cut from
116 squares cut 2⅜"
96 D ☐ squares cut 2"

YARDAGE & CUTTING, *continued*

8¾ yards White or Cream:
2 borders** cut 6½" x 96½"
2 borders** cut 6½" x 84½"
2 borders** cut 8" x 69½"
2 borders** cut 8" x 54½"
24 E ⬡ prisms* cut from
24 rectangles** cut 3½" x 12½"
20 H ☐ rectangles** cut 5" x 9½"
4 J ☐ rectangles** cut 2" x 8"
20 I ☐ rectangles** cut 2" x 6½"
116 C ⊠ quarter-square triangles cut
from 29 squares cut 4¼"
4 A ☐ squares cut 3½"
16 G △ half prisms* cut from
16 squares cut 3½"
24 F ☐ rectangles** cut 2" x 3½"
544 B ◺ half-square triangles cut from
272 squares cut 2⅜"
252 D ☐ squares cut 2"

9¼ yards 44"-Wide Backing Fabric:
3 panels cut 35¼" x 104½"

¾ yard Binding Fabric:
2" x 394"

---

*See the cutting directions for the E prisms and G half prisms on page 15.

If you wish to use strip piecing for the D-D units, or use your favorite Flying Geese method, you may require a little extra yardage of all three colors.

**Rotary cut rectangles for E, F, H, I, and J and borders with the long edges on the lengthwise grain of the fabric.

Be sure to read the material at the front of the book that explains my method, identifies exactly what I include in my dimensions and yardage figures, teaches you how to get the most out of the diagrams, and details how to rotary cut and piece the Evening Star blocks.

Rotary cut the longest borders first, cutting parallel to the selvage. Then cut the shorter borders and the largest patches. They are listed in size order. Cut smaller patches from the leftovers.

For this pattern, I strongly recommend trimming the points on the red B triangles in order to help you align the patches for piecing. Use the A trim on my Point Trimmer tool, or download the charts and

instructions for using your regular ruler to trim the points by going to the RWB Extras page at
judymartin.com

If you wish, you can eliminate dogears by also trimming the points of the remaining B triangles and all C triangles. Use the A trim of my tool or the downloaded A chart to trim the points of the B triangles; use the B trim for the C triangles.

You need not cut everything before you start sewing. You can cut a little and sew a little, if you like. If you plan to do that, start by cutting off a 4¾-yard length of white or cream for the borders and set it aside. Then use the remaining yardage to cut the patches you intend to sew first.

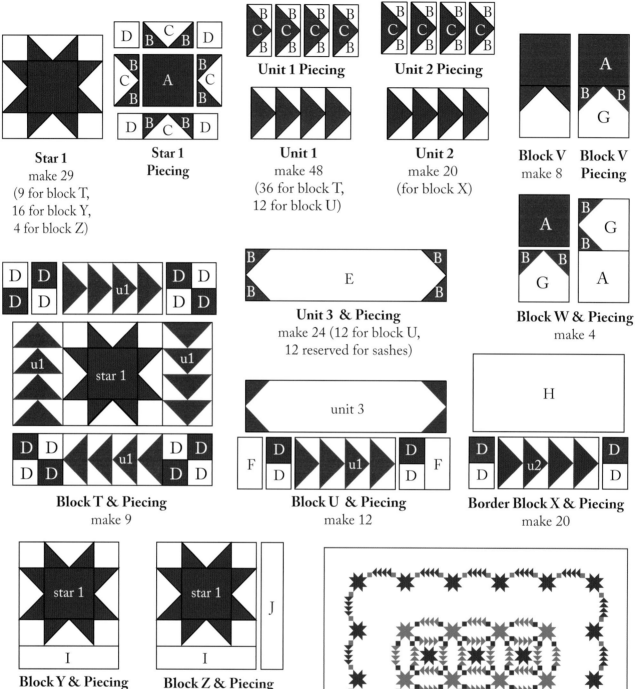

Star 1
make 29
(9 for block T,
16 for block Y,
4 for block Z)

**Star 1
Piecing**

Unit 1 Piecing

Unit 2 Piecing

Unit 1
make 48
(36 for block T,
12 for block U)

Unit 2
make 20
(for block X)

Block V
make 8

**Block V
Piecing**

Block W & Piecing
make 4

Unit 3 & Piecing
make 24 (12 for block U,
12 reserved for sashes)

Block T & Piecing
make 9

Block U & Piecing
make 12

Border Block X & Piecing
make 20

Block Y & Piecing
make 16

Block Z & Piecing
make 4

Make star 1's and units 1–3 in the quantities shown above. Use these units to make blocks T–Z in the quantities shown. You will have 12 leftover unit 3's to use for the sashing.

For this version of July Fireworks, substitute medium blue for red in the diagrams, cutting lists and yardage.

JULY FIREWORKS QUILT CONSTRUCTION

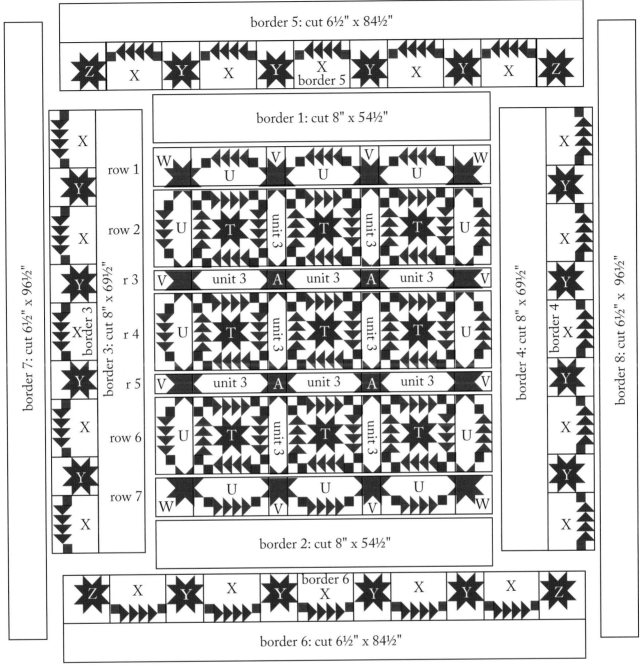

July Fireworks Whole Quilt Construction

Note that you must take care to turn blocks as shown above. For row 1 of the quilt center, join 3 U blocks alternately with 2 V blocks; add a W to each end. Repeat for the bottom row.

For row 2, join 3 T blocks alternately with 2 unit 3's; add a U to each end. Repeat for rows 4 and 6.

For row 3, join 3 unit 3's alternately with 2 red A squares; add a V block to each end. Repeat for row 5.

Join rows as shown. Add the 54½"-long top and bottom plain borders to complete the quilt center.

For the left border, join 5 X blocks alternately with 4 Y blocks as shown; attach a 69½" border to the

starry edge. Repeat for the right border. Attach these to the sides of the quilt, with the pieced borders on the outside edges.

For the top border, join 5 X blocks alternately with 4 Y's, with stars touching one long edge and Flying Geese touching the other. Add a Z block to each end, turned as shown above. Attach an 84½" border to the outside edge, orienting blocks as shown. Repeat for the bottom border. Stitch the top and bottom borders to the quilt, as shown above. Attach the remaining two 96½" borders to the left and right sides to complete the quilt top.

53

RISE & SHINE: RED, WHITE & BLUE

Rise & Shine, 65½" x 65½", pieced and quilted by Sally Yakish. This quilt, with its unique star sashing, yields remarkably different results depending on whether the stars or their backgrounds (or some of each) are white. I present patterns for three versions: one patriotic, one blue and white, and one red and cream. Each is presented with its own specifications and diagrams because the changes are such that one color does not directly substitute for another. An additional variation is shown on page 18. For this, you can use the specifications and diagrams for the patriotic version above and simply substitute navy for red in the diagrams. Also add the red yardage amount and cutting list to the navy.

I designed Rise & Shine in 2020 for this book. I devised the sashing from units rather than individual star blocks in order to minimize the number of patches and simplify the joints.

The patriotic version is an appropriate size and coloring for a Quilt of Valor®.

Sally used a single white fabric, two red fabrics, and an assortment of blues. If you wish to use scraps throughout, you can piece the blue border strips (and/or the white K's) from 18" lengths of a number of fat quarters. If you wish to use 2 reds, as Sally did, buy ⅝ yard for the big I and J triangles in the unit 7's and ¼ yard (or 1 fat quarter) for the E triangles in the Z blocks.

RED, WHITE & BLUE RISE & SHINE SPECIFICATIONS

Quilt Size: 65½" x 65½"
Block Size: 12" Z
Star Sizes: 6" and 12"
Requires: 4 star 1, 4 Z, 34 unit 1, 53 unit 2, 36 unit 3, 10 unit 4, 3 unit 5, 4 unit 6, 4 unit 7

YARDAGE & CUTTING

2½ yards or 11 fat quarters Navy Blue:
4 borders** cut 3½" x 66¾"* (mitered)
156 C ⊠ quarter-square triangles cut from 39 squares cut 4¼"
72 H ▭ rectangles** cut 2" x 3½"
36 G □ squares cut 2⅝"
84 D □ squares cut 2"

¾ yard or 4 or more fat quarters Red:
4 J ◣ half-square triangles cut from 2 squares cut 12⅞"
8 I ◣ half-square triangles cut from 4 squares cut 6⅞"
32 E ◣ half-square triangles cut from 16 squares cut 3⅞"

2⅞ yards or 12 fat quarters White:
8 K ◣▱ trapezoids* cut from 8 rectangles** cut 3⅜" x 31"
16 F ⊠ quarter-square triangles cut from 4 squares cut 7¼"
73 A □ squares cut 3½"
456 B ◣ half-square triangles cut from 228 squares cut 2⅜"

4⅜ yards 44"-Wide Backing Fabric:
2 panels cut 37¼" x 74"

½ yard Binding Fabric:
2" x 272"

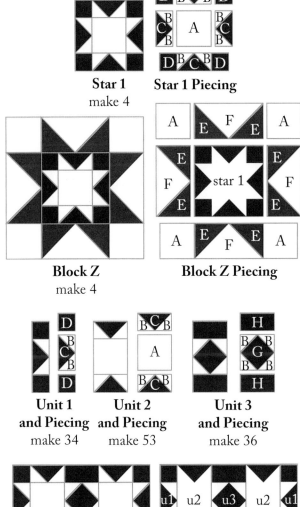

Star 1
make 4

Star 1 Piecing

Block Z
make 4

Block Z Piecing

Unit 1 and Piecing
make 34

Unit 2 and Piecing
make 53

Unit 3 and Piecing
make 36

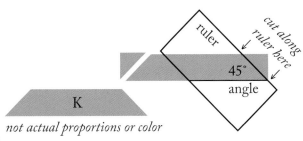

Unit 4
make 10

Unit 4 Piecing

Make 4 star 1's and use them to make 4 block Z's. Also make units 1–3 in the quantities listed above. Use some of these to make 10 unit 4's as shown here.

See the notes for all versions on the bottom of page 57.

***Rotary cut rectangles for H and K and borders with the long edges on the lengthwise grain of the fabric.*

**Cut trapezoids for K and mitered borders as shown below.*

For K trapezoids and outer borders, cut rectangles of the listed size: 3⅜" x 31" for K's and 3½" x 66¾" for borders. Cut off both ends of each at a 45-degree angle as shown at right. The 45-degree line should be precisely aligned with the corner. Cut along the ruler's edge to remove a waste triangle at one corner. Repeat at the opposite end to make a trapezoid. Both points need to be on the same long edge.

ruler
cut along ruler here
45° angle
K

not actual proportions or color

Unit 5 and Piecing
make 3

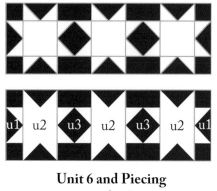

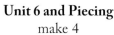

Unit 6 and Piecing
make 4

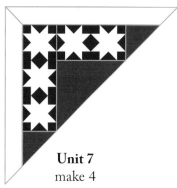

Unit 7
make 4

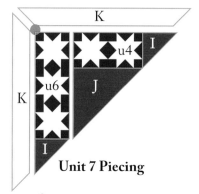

Unit 7 Piecing

MITERING INSTRUCTIONS: ALL 3 VERSIONS

To complete unit 7 (or unit 11 of the blue-and-white version on page 59), attach the 2 K trapezoids to the unit starting at the pink dot ¼" inch in from the raw edges at the square corner of the unit. Stitch from this point to the raw edge at the opposite end for each K. Leave the miter joining the 2 K's to each other unstitched until you have

sewn the rest of the quilt, including adding the outer borders. Start stitching the miter at the pink dot in the diagram. It indicates the exact point where you started stitching the 2 K's to the unit 7 (or unit 11 on page 59). Stitch the miter all the way through the border corners, matching the seams that join the K's to the borders.

Use the remaining units 1–3 to make 3 unit 5's and 4 unit 6's, as shown above. Use 4 of the unit 4's and 4 unit 6's to make 4 unit 7's as follows: Stitch a unit 4 to an I and a J triangle as shown for unit 7. Stitch another I triangle to a unit 6. Join the two parts to form a triangle. Add 2 K trapezoids to complete unit 7, as described above in italic. Leave the miter unstitched for now. Make 4 unit 7's.

See the diagram at the right. Sew 3 unit 4's alternately with 2 Z's to make a block row. Repeat. Join 3 unit 5's alternately with these 2 block rows to complete the diagonal quilt center. Attach a unit 7 to each side of the quilt center. Cut off both ends of each blue border strip at a 45-degree angle as described on the bottom of page 55. Stitch a blue border to each side of the quilt. Miter the corners of the K's and borders as described in italic, above.

Quilt as desired and bind to finish.

Rise & Shine Whole Quilt Construction: Red, White & Blue

RISE & SHINE: BLUE & WHITE

I pieced the blue-and-white version of Rise & Shine. Debbi Treusch quilted it. An additional blue-and-white variation is shown on page 18. Of course, you can easily substitute red for the blue if you prefer warm colors. I *made this quilt entirely from my stash. If you like the scrappy look, you can piece the borders from 18" lengths of assorted fat quarters if you don't have long, narrow remnants in your stash for the cream K's and blue borders.*

RISE & SHINE NOTES: ALL VERSIONS

For all versions of Rise & Shine, read the material at the front of the book that explains my method, identifies exactly what I include in my dimensions and yardage figures, teaches you how to get the most out of the diagrams, and details how to rotary cut and piece the Rising Star and Evening Star blocks.

Cut the borders first, cutting parallel to the selvage. Then cut the largest patches. They are listed in size order. Cut smaller patches from the leftovers.

You need not cut everything before you start sewing. You can cut a little and sew a little, if you like.

In order to help you align the patches for piecing, I strongly recommend trimming the points on the I triangles, K trapezoids, and the B triangles that are sewn to G squares. Use the C trim on my Point Trimmer tool, or download the file and instructions for making your own point trimming guide by going to the RWB Extras page at judymartin.com

If you wish, you can eliminate dogears by also trimming the points of the remaining B triangles and all C, E, F, and J triangles. For the B, E and J triangles use the A trim of my tool or your downloaded file; for the C and F triangles, use the B trim. Download charts and instructions for using your regular ruler to trim the points by going to the RWB Extras page at judymartin.com

BLUE & WHITE RISE & SHINE SPECIFICATIONS

Quilt Size: 65½" x 65½"
Block Size: 12" Z
Star Sizes: 6" and 12"
Requires: 4 star 1, 4 Z, 18 unit 1,
   33 unit 2, 24 unit 3, 6 unit 4, 3 unit 5,
   16 unit 6, 20 unit 7, 12 unit 8, 4 unit 9,
   4 unit 10, 4 unit 11

YARDAGE & CUTTING

2⅞ yards or 12 fat quarters Navy Blue:
4 borders** cut 3½" x 66¾"* (mitered)
100 C ⊠ quarter-square triangles cut
   from 25 squares cut 4¼"
32 E ◺ half-square triangles cut from
   16 squares cut 3⅞"
20 A ☐ squares cut 3½"
48 H ▭ rectangles** cut 2" x 3½"
24 G ☐ squares cut 2⅝"
160 B ◺ half-square triangles cut from
   80 squares cut 2⅜"
52 D ☐ squares cut 2"

3¼ yards or 14 fat quarters Cream:
8 K ⬠ trapezoids* cut from
   8 rectangles** cut 3⅜" x 31"
4 J ◺ half-square triangles cut from
   2 squares cut 12⅞"
16 F ⊠ quarter-square triangles cut from
   4 squares cut 7¼"
8 I ◺ half-square triangles cut from
   4 squares cut 6⅞"
56 C ⊠ quarter-square triangles cut from
   14 squares cut 4¼"
53 A ☐ squares cut 3½"
24 H ▭ rectangles** cut 2" x 3½"
12 G ☐ squares cut 2⅝"
296 B ◺ half-square triangles cut from
   148 squares cut 2⅜"
32 D ☐ squares cut 2"

4⅜ yards 44"-Wide Backing Fabric:
2 panels cut 37¼" x 74"

½ yard Binding Fabric:
2" x 272"

*Cut trapezoids for K and mitered borders as shown on page 55.

**Rotary cut rectangles for H and K and borders with the long edges on the lengthwise grain of the fabric.

See the notes for all versions on page 57.

RISE & SHINE STARS, BLOCKS & UNITS: BLUE & WHITE

Star 1
make 4

Star 1 Piecing

Block Z
make 4

Block Z Piecing

Unit 1 and Piecing
make 18

Unit 2 and Piecing
make 33

Unit 3 and Piecing
make 24

Unit 4
make 6

Unit 4 Piecing

Make 4 star 1's as shown above, and use them to make 4 block Z's. Also make 18 unit 1's, 33 unit 2's, and 24 unit 3's. Use these to make 6 unit 4's, shown above, and 3 unit 5's, shown on the next page.

58

Unit 5 and Piecing
make 3

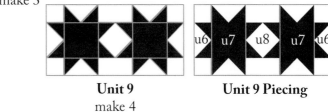

**Unit 6
and Piecing**
make 16

**Unit 7
and Piecing**
make 20

**Unit 8
and Piecing**
make 12

Unit 9
make 4

Unit 9 Piecing

Unit 10 and Piecing
make 4

Unit 11
make 4

Unit 11 Piecing

Following the diagrams above, make 16 unit 6's, 20 unit 7's, and 12 unit 8's. Use these to make 4 unit 9's and 4 unit 10's. Stitch a unit 9 to an I and a J triangle as shown for unit 11. Stitch another I triangle to a unit 10. Join the two parts to form a triangle. Add 2 K trapezoids to complete unit 11, as described in italic on page 56. Leave the miter unstitched for now. Make 4 unit 11's.

Referring to the quilt diagram at right, sew 3 unit 4's alternately with 2 Z's to make a block row. Repeat to make a second block row. Join 3 unit 5's alternately with 2 block rows to complete the diagonal quilt center.

Stitch a unit 11 to each side of the quilt center.

Cut off both ends of each border strip at a 45-degree angle as shown at the bottom of page 55. Stitch a border to each side of the quilt. Miter the corners of K's and borders as described in italic on page 56.

Quilt and bind to finish.

Rise & Shine Whole Quilt Construction: Blue & White

RISE & SHINE INSTRUCTIONS: RED & WHITE

RED & WHITE RISE & SHINE QUILT SPECIFICATIONS

Quilt Size: 65½" x 65½"
Block Size: 12" Z
Star Sizes: 6" and 12"
Requires: 4 star 1, 4 Z, 34 unit 1,
53 unit 2, 36 unit 3, 10 unit 4, 3 unit 5,
4 unit 6, 4 unit 7

YARDAGE & CUTTING

3¼ yards or 14 fat quarters Cream:
8 K ⬭ trapezoids* cut from
8 rectangles** cut 3⅜" x 31"
4 J ◺ half-square triangles cut from
2 squares cut 12⅞"
16 F ⊠ quarter-square triangles cut from
4 squares cut 7¼"
8 I ◺ half-square triangles cut from
4 squares cut 6⅞"
156 C ⊠ quarter-square triangles cut
from 39 squares cut 4¼"
16 A ☐ squares cut 3½"
72 H ▭ rectangles** cut 2" x 3½"
36 G ☐ squares cut 2⅝"
84 D ☐ squares cut 2"

2¾ yards or 12 fat quarters Red:
4 borders** cut 3½" x 66¾"* (mitered)
32 E ◺ half-square triangles cut from
16 squares cut 3⅞"
57 A ☐ squares cut 3½"
456 B ◺ half-square triangles cut from
228 squares cut 2⅜"

4⅜ yards 44"-Wide Backing Fabric:
2 panels cut 37¼" x 74"

½ yard Binding Fabric:
2" x 272"

Cut trapezoids for K and borders as shown on page 55.

**Rotary cut rectangles for H and K and borders with the long edges on the lengthwise grain of the fabric.*

If you are using fat quarters, you can piece the K's and borders from 18" lengths of various fat quarters.

See the notes for all versions on the bottom of page 57.

Red and White Version of Rise & Shine

RISE & SHINE STAR 1 & BLOCK Z: RED & WHITE

Star 1
make 4

Star 1 Piecing

Block Z
make 4

Block Z Piecing

Make 4 star 1's as shown above. Use them to make 4 block Z's.

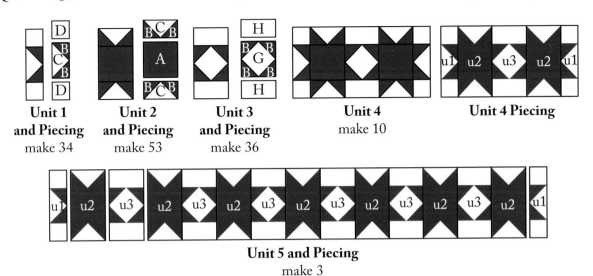

Unit 1 and Piecing make 34

Unit 2 and Piecing make 53

Unit 3 and Piecing make 36

Unit 4 make 10

Unit 4 Piecing

Unit 5 and Piecing make 3

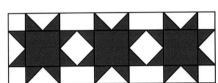

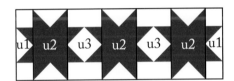

Unit 6 and Piecing make 4

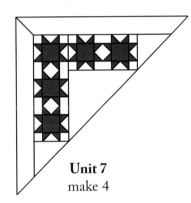

Unit 7 make 4

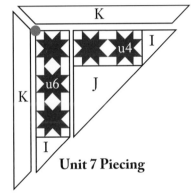

Unit 7 Piecing

Make units 1–3 as shown above. Use these to make units 4, 5, and 6. Use units 4 and 6 to make 4 unit 7's. Start by stitching a unit 4 to an I and a J triangle as shown. Stitch another I triangle to a unit 6. Join the two parts to form a triangle. Add 2 K trapezoids to complete unit 7, as described in italic on page 56. Leave the miter unstitched for now. Make 4 unit 7's.

See the whole quilt diagram at right. Sew 3 unit 4's alternately with 2 Z's to make a block row. Repeat. Join 3 unit 5's alternately with 2 block rows to complete the diagonal quilt center.

Attach a unit 7 to each side of the quilt center.

Cut off both ends of each red border strip at a 45-degree angle as shown on page 55. Stitch a border to each side of the quilt. Miter the corners of K's and borders together, as described in italic on page 56.

Quilt and bind to finish.

Rise & Shine Whole Quilt Construction: Red & White

STARS 'N' STRIPES FOREVER

Stars'n' Stripes Forever, 72" x 89", pieced by Mary Bird in 2020 and quilted by Vicki Bales.

I designed this quilt on September 11, 2001. I planned it specifically to go with the border, which I designed in 1994 for Pieced Borders. The quilt pattern was first published as a Block of the Month on my web site. A slight variation appeared in Knockout Blocks & Sampler Quilts in 2004.

Mary made her quilt from just three fabrics. If you want to make your quilt from scraps, I suggest you sort the scraps to match pretty closely, especially in the red H, I, and J triangles that square off the quilt center and inner edge of the pieced border.

A decidedly different 2-color variation is on page 21. The color substitutions are not direct, so you will need to do some figuring to make that version. The charts on page 17 will help with the changes.

I changed the width of the plain border for this book in order to make it an appropriate size for an official Quilt of Valor®.

STARS 'N' STRIPES FOREVER INSTRUCTIONS

QUILT SPECIFICATIONS

Quilt Size: 72" x 89"
Block Size: 12" X, 6" W, Y, and Z
Star Sizes: 6" and 12"
Requires: 48 W, 8 X, 32 Y, 14 Z,
  2 unit 1, 2 unit 2, 4 unit 3, 2 unit 4,
  2 unit 5, 2 unit 6, 8 unit 7, 6 unit 8,
  2 unit 9, 4 unit 10

YARDAGE & CUTTING

2½ yards or 10 fat quarters Navy Blue:
32 H ⊠ quarter-square triangles cut from
  8 squares cut 9¾"
4 I ◺ half-square triangles cut from
  2 squares cut 5⅛"
192 C ⊠ quarter-square triangles cut
  from 48 squares cut 4¼"
304 D ☐ squares cut 2"

3 yards or 12 fat quarters Red:
2 borders* cut 2½" x 85½"**
2 borders* cut 2½" x 72½"**
40 H ⊠ quarter-square triangles cut from
  10 squares cut 9¾"

Red, *continued*
4 J ◺ half-square triangles cut from
  2 squares cut 9⅜"
4 I ◺ half-square triangles cut from
  2 squares cut 5⅛"
64 G ☐ rectangles* cut 2" x 6½"
64 E ◺ half-square triangles cut from
  32 squares cut 3⅞"

3¼ yds. or 13 fat qtrs. White or Cream:
32 F ⊠ quarter-square triangles cut from
  8 squares cut 7¼"
64 G ☐ rectangles* cut 2" x 6½"
80 A ☐ squares cut 3½"
384 B ◺ half-square triangles cut from
  192 squares cut 2⅜"
112 D ☐ squares cut 2"

5¾ yards 44"-Wide Backing Fabric:
2 panels cut 40½" x 97½"

½ yard Binding Fabric:
2" x 332"

Rotary cut G rectangles and borders with the long edges on the lengthwise grain of the fabric.

**If you use fat quarters for the red, you can piece the border strips from 17"-18" lengths cut from fat quarters.*

Be sure to read the material at the front of the book that explains my method, identifies exactly what I include in my dimensions and yardage figures, teaches you how to get the most out of the diagrams, and details how to rotary cut and piece the Rising Star and Evening Star blocks.

Rotary cut the longest borders first, cutting parallel to the selvage. Then cut the shorter borders and the largest patches. They are listed in size order. Cut smaller patches from the leftovers.

If you are using scraps or fat quarters, you can piece the borders from 2½" x 17" or 2½" x 18" strips of numerous similarly colored fat quarters.

You need not cut everything before you start sewing. You can cut a little and sew a little, if you like. If you plan to do that from yardage, start by cutting off an 86" length from the red yardage to reserve for the borders and set it aside. Then use the remainder to cut the red patches you intend to sew first.

I strongly recommend trimming the points on the H, I, and J triangles in order to help you align the patches for piecing. Use the C trim on my Point Trimmer tool, or download the file and instructions for making your own C point trimmer by going to the RWB Extras page at
judymartin.com

If you wish, you can eliminate dogears by also trimming the points of the B, C, E, and F triangles. For the B, and E triangles, use the A trim of my tool or your downloaded file; for the C and F triangles, use the B trim. Download charts and instructions for using your regular ruler to trim these points by going to the RWB Extras page at
judymartin.com

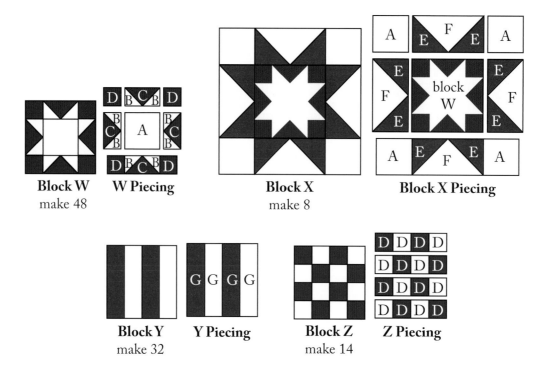

Block W
make 48

W Piecing

Block X
make 8

Block X Piecing

Block Y
make 32

Y Piecing

Block Z
make 14

Z Piecing

Press the seams of the Y blocks toward the red end. Press the seam allowances between **patches** within a row of a Z block toward the blue end. Press the seam allowances of the Z block **rows** toward the bottom of the block when it is oriented as shown in the Z block diagram, above right.

When joining blocks to make border units 5 and 6, turn the Z blocks so that the Z **row** seam allowances and Y seam allowances oppose each other and the red stripes

touch the white squares. In units 7 and 9, turn Z's so the seams between the Z **patches** oppose the seams of the Y blocks. That way, when the units are joined to make the borders, the seam allowances of the Y and Z blocks naturally oppose. Press the seam allowances joining Y's to Z blocks toward the Y's. Press the seam allowances within border units away from the stars and toward the red and blue H, I, and J triangles wherever possible.

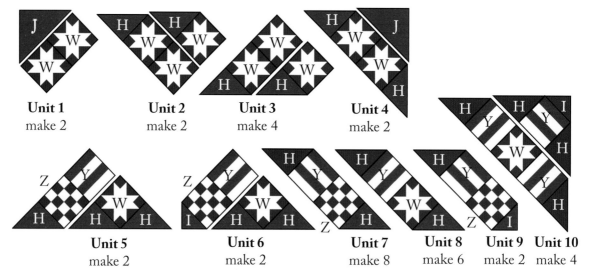

Unit 1
make 2

Unit 2
make 2

Unit 3
make 4

Unit 4
make 2

Unit 5
make 2

Unit 6
make 2

Unit 7
make 8

Unit 8
make 6

Unit 9
make 2

Unit 10
make 4

Note that the 48 W blocks include those in X blocks and in border units 1–6, 8, and 10.

If you prefer to strip piece blocks Y and Z, I recommend cutting lengthwise strips for a more stable grain (and more scrap variety if you are using scraps). You may need slightly more yardage for strip piecing, as there may be waste at the end of the strip set

after cutting. All of the Y and Z blocks are used in border units, as shown above.

Make blocks and units in the quantities listed. Units 1–6 and 10 are exploded to show diagonal rows. Sew the two segments together to complete each of these units before sewing the units to each other and to the quilt.

STARS 'N' STRIPES FOREVER QUILT CONSTRUCTION

Stars 'n' Stripes Forever Whole Quilt Construction

After completing all blocks and units, start the quilt assembly with the quilt center. This is made from two identical halves. For the top half, sew three X blocks together in a diagonal row. Add a unit 1 to the upper left end and a unit 3 to the lower right end. Make another diagonal row by joining a unit 2 to the upper left of an X block; then sew a unit 3 to the lower right end; sew a unit 4 to the upper right side of this row. Add the row with 3 X blocks to this section to complete the top half of the quilt center.

Make the bottom half exactly the same. (When you rotate the completed bottom half 180 degrees, you will see this matches the quilt diagram.) Join halves to complete the quilt center.

As you add borders, press them away from the quilt center. Left and right borders are identical. Join 2 unit 8's alternately with 2 unit 7's; add unit 9 to the unit 8 end; add unit 6 to the unit 7 end. Attach to the left side of the quilt. Repeat for the right side.

The top and bottom borders are identical. Join units 5-7-8-7 in diagonal rows as shown at the top of the diagram. Attach this to the top of the quilt. Repeat for the bottom.

The four corners of the quilt borders are identical. Sew a unit 10 to each corner of the quilt.

Attach the 85½"-long red borders to the two long sides of the quilt. Finally, attach the two shorter red borders to the top and bottom to complete the top.

65

STAR-SPANGLED QUILT: 2 SIZES

Star-Spangled Quilt, 64" x 88" (above) and 40" x 40" (at right) were pieced by Marilyn Deppe and quilted by Carol Westercamp in 2021. The larger size is ideal for a twin bed or a TV quilt for two to snuggle under. It is also appropriate for a Quilt of Valor®. The one-block version makes a quick little wall quilt or table topper to brighten your Independence Day.

I designed the 24" Star-Spangled Quilt block for my 1998 book, The Block Book. I added the plain borders with an asymmetrical corner treatment for this book.

A red-and-white version of this is shown on page 18. It is an easy matter of adding the navy yardage and cutting list to the red to make the changes to the pattern.

STAR-SPANGLED QUILT INSTRUCTIONS IN 2 SIZES

TWIN QUILT SPECIFICATIONS

Quilt Size: 64" x 88"
Block Size: 24" Y blocks, 8" Z blocks
Star Size: 8"
Requires: 6 Y, 2 Z, 6 unit 1, 24 unit 2

YARDAGE & CUTTING

1½ yards or 6 fat quarters Navy Blue:
32 A ☐ squares cut 4½"
256 B ◺ half-square triangles cut from
   128 squares cut 2⅞"

⅞ yard or 4 fat quarters Red:
48 F ▭ rectangles** cut 1½" x 12½"

4¾ yards White:
2 borders** cut 8½" x 72½"
2 borders** cut 8½" x 56½"
48 F ▭ rectangles** cut 1½" x 12½"
24 G ▭ rectangles** cut 2½" x 6½"
80 C ⊠ quarter-square triangles cut from
   20 squares cut 5¼"
48 E △ half prisms* cut from
   48 squares cut 4½"
56 D ☐ squares cut 2½"

5¾ yards 44"-Wide Backing Fabric:
2 panels cut 36½" x 96½"

½ yard Binding Fabric:
2" x 314"

WALL QUILT SPECIFICATIONS

Quilt Size: 40" x 40"
Block Size: 24" Y blocks, 8" Z blocks
Star Size: 8"
Requires: 1 Y, 2 Z, 1 unit 1, 4 unit 2

YARDAGE & CUTTING

⅜ yard or 2 or more fat quarters Navy:
7 A ☐ squares cut 4½"
56 B ◺ half-square triangles cut from
   28 squares cut 2⅞"

⅜ yard or 1 or more fat quarters Red:
8 F ▭ rectangles** cut 1½" x 12½"

1½ yards White:
2 borders** cut 8½" x 32½"
2 borders** cut 8½" x 24½"
8 F ▭ rectangles** cut 1½" x 12½"
4 G ▭ rectangles** cut 2½" x 6½"
20 C ⊠ quarter-square triangles cut from
   5 squares cut 5¼"
8 E △ half prisms* cut from
   8 squares cut 4½"
16 D ☐ squares cut 2½"

3 yards 44"-Wide Backing Fabric:
2 panels cut 24½" x 48½"

½ yard Binding Fabric:
2" x 170"

Cut E half prisms as shown on page 15.

**For more stable grain, cut the F and G rectangles and borders with their long sides on the lengthwise grain of the fabric.*

The five stars of the 24" block were designed not as individual blocks, but as units that simplify the piecing of the elements. You can rotary cut the house-shaped E patches using my multi-purpose Shapemaker 45 tool. If you prefer, you can make your own rotary cutting guide by downloading a file from my website and following its directions. Go to the RWB Extras page at judymartin.com

Read the material at the front of the book that identifies exactly what I include in my dimensions and yardage figures, tells how to get the most out of the diagrams, and details how to rotary cut and piece the Evening Star blocks.

   Rotary cut the borders first, cutting parallel to the selvage. Then cut the largest patches. They are listed in size order. Cut smaller patches from the leftovers. You need not cut everything before you start sewing. Just cut a little and sew a little, if you like.

   For this pattern, I strongly recommend trimming the points of the blue B triangles in order to help you align the patches for piecing. Use the A trim on my Point Trimmer tool, or download the charts and instructions for using your regular ruler to trim the points by going to the RWB Extras page at judymartin.com

   If you wish, eliminate dogears by also trimming the points of the C triangles. Use the B trim of my tool or the downloaded B chart for the C triangles.

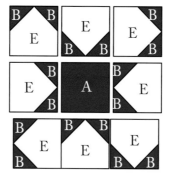

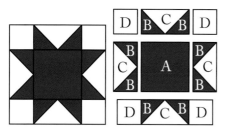

Block Z & Piecing
make 2 Twin/Throw
or rmake 2 Wall

Unit 1 & Piecing
make 6 Twin/Throw
or make 1 Wall

Unit 2 & Piecing
make 24 Twin/Throw
or make 4 Wall

Block Y
make 6 Twin/Throw
or make 1 Wall

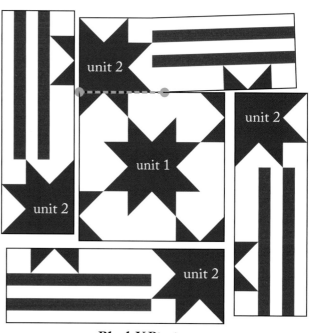

Block Y Piecing

For Block Y, start by attaching the top unit 2 to the unit 1 with a partial seam, indicated in green above. Begin stitching at the left green dot and end at about the right green dot. Add the left unit 2, then the bottom and right unit 2's. Finally, stitch the rest of the seamline for the top unit 2.

Make Z blocks for the border corners, and make units 1 and 2 in the quantities listed above for your chosen quilt size.

Use units 1 and 2 to make Y blocks in the quantity listed. Note the directions in italic, above, for making a partial seam when you start to assemble the block.

For the blue-and-white version at right, substitute blue for white and white for both red and blue in diagrams. Add together the red and blue yardges and cutting lists to get the white totals.

STAR-SPANGLED QUILT CONSTRUCTION: 2 QUILT SIZES

border 3: cut 8½" x 56½"

border 1: cut 8½" x 72½"

border 2: cut 8½" x 72½"

border 4: cut 8½" x 56½"

Whole Quilt Construction: Twin/Throw Size

Assemble the twin/throw quilt as shown at left. Join 3 blocks in a vertical column. Repeat. Sew the two columns together.

Attach the longer white borders to the right and left sides of the quilt. Sew a Z block to one end of each remaining border. Turn the borders as shown, and stitch to the top and bottom of the quilt.

Quilt as desired and bind the quilt to finish.

Assemble the table topper/wall quilt as shown at right. Stitch the shorter white borders to the left and right sides of the Y block. Sew a Z block to one end of each remaining border. Turn the borders as shown, and stitch to the top and bottom of the quilt.

Quilt as desired and bind to finish.

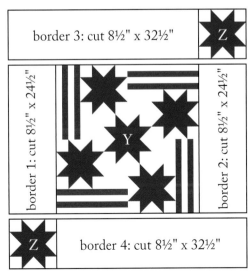

border 3: cut 8½" x 32½"

border 1: cut 8½" x 24½"

border 2: cut 8½" x 24½"

border 4: cut 8½" x 32½"

Whole Quilt Construction: Wall Size

69

STAR BRIGHT

Star Bright, 98" x 98", pieced by Chris Hulin and quilted by Carol Westercamp. The central 9 blocks and sashes plus the top border fit the top surface of a queen bed perfectly, and the pieced borders handsomely drape down the sides and bottom.

I designed the Star Bright quilt in 2019 for this book. I took inspiration for the sashing from my Maritime quilt (Stellar Quilts, 2010), though I changed the pieced setting squares where the sashes meet. The pieced borders were inspired by my Anniversary Stars quilt (Quilter's Newsletter, 2014). I changed the larger border star to a Rising Star here to echo the quilt center.

Though the border looks more complex than a border of similar stars side by side, this one is easier to sew. The different star sizes mean you have no joints to match when you sew the blocks together.

Be sure to see the patriotic version of Star Bright on page 19. Simply substitute red for medium blue.

QUILT SPECIFICATIONS

Quilt Size: 98" x 98"

Block Size: 6" U, 12" V and W,
8" x 12" X, 6" x 12" Y and Z sashes

Star Sizes: 6", 8", 12"

Requires: 21 star 1, 20 star 2, 16 U, 21 V,
4 W, 16 X, 16 Y, 8 Z

YARDAGE & CUTTING

2¼ yards or 9 fat quarters Navy Blue:

24 N ☐ rectangles* cut 1½" x 12½"
16 R ☐ rectangles* cut 1½" x 6½"
20 G ☐ squares cut 4½"
16 Q ☐ rectangles* cut 1½" x 4½"
84 C ⊠ quarter-square triangles cut from
21 squares cut 4¼"
16 P ☐ rectangles* cut 1½" x 3½"
160 H ◺ half-square triangles cut from
80 squares cut 2⅞"
84 D ☐ squares cut 2"
16 S ☐ squares cut 1½"

2 yards or 8 fat quarters Medium Blue:

24 N ☐ rectangles* cut 1½" x 12½"
16 R ☐ rectangles* cut 1½" x 6½"
16 Q ☐ rectangles* cut 1½" x 4½"
168 E ◺ half-square triangles cut from
84 squares cut 3⅞"
16 P ☐ rectangles* cut 1½" x 3½"
16 S ☐ squares cut 1½"

YARDAGE & CUTTING, continued

8 yards White or Cream:

2 borders* cut 3½" x 98½"
2 borders* cut 3½" x 92½"
2 borders* cut 4½" x 68½"
2 borders* cut 4½" x 60½"
24 M ☐ rectangles* cut 3½" x 12½"
8 L ☐ rectangles* cut 2½" x 12½"
24 N ☐ rectangles* cut 1½" x 12½"
40 K ☐ rectangles* cut 2½" x 8½"
84 F ⊠ quarter-square triangles cut from
21 squares cut 7¼"
80 I ⊠ quarter-square triangles cut from
20 squares cut 5¼"
105 A ☐ squares cut 3½"
80 J ☐ squares cut 2½"
168 B ◺ half-square triangles cut from
84 squares cut 2⅜"
32 O ☐ rectangles* cut 1½" x 2½"
64 S ☐ squares cut 1½"

9⅜ yards 44"-Wide Backing Fabric:

3 panels cut 35⅞" x 106½"

¾ yard Binding Fabric:

2" x 402"

For more stable grain, cut the K, L, M, N, O, P, Q, and R rectangles and borders with the long sides on the lengthwise grain of the fabric.

Read the material at the front of the book that identifies exactly what I include in my dimensions and yardage figures, tells how to get the most out of the diagrams, and details how to rotary cut and piece the Rising Star and Evening Star blocks.

Rotary cut the borders first, cutting parallel to the selvage. Then cut the largest patches. They are listed in size order. Cut smaller patches from the leftovers. You need not cut everything before you start sewing. Just cut a little and sew a little, if you like.

If you wish, you can eliminate dogears by trimming the points of the B, C, E, F, H, and I triangles. Use my Point Trimmer tool or download charts and instructions for using your regular ruler to trim points by going to the RWB Extras page at
judymartin.com

For the B, E, and H triangles use the A trim of my tool or the downloaded A chart; for the C, F, and I triangles, use the B trim of my tool or the downloaded B chart.

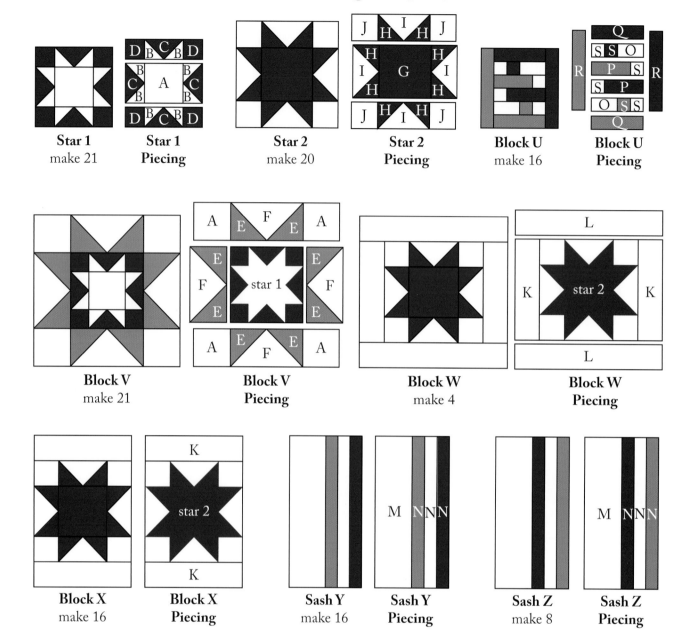

Star 1
make 21

Star 1 Piecing

Star 2
make 20

Star 2 Piecing

Block U
make 16

Block U Piecing

Block V
make 21

Block V Piecing

Block W
make 4

Block W Piecing

Block X
make 16

Block X Piecing

Sash Y
make 16

Sash Y Piecing

Sash Z
make 8

Sash Z Piecing

See the information about making Rising Star and Evening Star blocks on pages 12–13. Make stars 1 and 2 and blocks U–Z in the quantities shown above. When making U setting squares and Y and Z sashes, be especially careful to place the medium blue and navy blue exactly as shown above.

Press seam allowances of stars and V blocks as shown on pages 12–13. Press seam allowances of blocks W and X away from the stars. Press seam allowances of block U away from the center. Press the seam allowances of the Y and Z sashes toward the cream M.

See the whole quilt diagram on the next page. Make the quilt center from sash rows and block rows, as shown. A sash row is made from blocks U/Y/U/Z/U/Y/U. Be careful to turn the U, Y, and Z blocks exactly as shown. Each sash row is made the same; every second sash rows is turned 180 degrees.

The top and bottom block rows are alike. Each has blocks Y/V/Y/W/Y/V/Y. Be careful to turn the Y blocks so the navy edges touch the W blocks.

The center row of blocks is made from blocks Z/W/Z/V/Z/W/Z. Be careful to turn the Z blocks so the medium blue edges touch the W blocks.

STAR BRIGHT QUILT CONSTRUCTION

Star Bright Whole Quilt Construction

Lay out the block and sash rows in the order and orientation shown above. Sew the rows together to complete the quilt center.

Add the 60½" plain borders to the right and left sides of the quilt center.

For the top pieced border, join X/V/X/V/X/V/X blocks. Stitch a 68½" border to one edge. Repeat for the bottom border. Attach these to the top and

bottom of the quilt, with the plain borders on the inside.

For the left border join V/X/V/X/V/X/V/X/V blocks. Stitch a 92½" border to one edge. Repeat for the right border. Attach these to the sides of the quilt, with the cream borders on the outside.

Add the 98½" plain borders to the top and bottom to complete the quilt. Quilt and bind to finish.

STARS IN STRIPES

Stars in Stripes, 65" x 84", pieced by Chris Hulin and quilted by Carol Westercamp. This patriotic strippy quilt makes a generous throw, a cheery kid's quilt or a handsome wall quilt.

I designed this quilt by combining the borders of several quilts from this book: Stars Over the States, Sparkler, and Star Bright/Military Band. I resized or reproportioned some of the elements to fit with each other in the strippy setting.

The red, white, and blue version shown here is sized appropriately for a Quilt of Valor®. I show Stars in Stripes in blues and white on page 19. For that version, substitute navy for bright blue and substitute medium blue for red in the yardage, specifications, and diagrams.

STARS IN STRIPES INSTRUCTIONS

QUILT SPECIFICATIONS

Quilt Size: 65" x 84"
Block Size: 8" U and V, 6" x 12" W, X, and Y, 12" Z
Star Sizes: 12", 8", and 6"
Requires: 4 star 1, 5 star 2, 14 star 3, 14 star 4, 8 U, 8 V, 14 W, 14 X, 4 Y, 5 Z

YARDAGE & CUTTING

1⅞ yards or 8 fat quarters Blue:
14 L ▭ rectangles* cut 5" x 6½"
14 K ▭ rectangles* cut 2" x 6½"
8 G ☐ squares cut 4½"
76 C ⊠ quarter-square triangles cut from 19 squares cut 4¼"
40 E ◺ half-square triangles cut from 20 squares cut 3⅞"
64 H ◺ half-square triangles cut from 32 squares cut 2⅞"
76 D ☐ squares cut 2"

1⅝ yards or 7 fat quarters Red:
14 L ▭ rectangles* cut 5" x 6½"
14 K ▭ rectangles* cut 2" x 6½"
8 G ☐ squares cut 4½"
56 C ⊠ quarter-square triangles cut from 14 squares cut 4¼"
4 A ☐ squares cut 3½"

Red Yardage & Cutting, *continued*
64 H ◺ half-square triangles cut from 32 squares cut 2⅞"
32 B ◺ half-square triangles cut from 16 squares cut 2⅜"
56 D ☐ squares cut 2"

4 yards White or Cream:
2 strips* cut 3½" x 84½"
2 strips* cut 2½" x 84½"
2 strips* cut 2" x 84½"
4 O ▭ rectangles* cut 3½" x 8½"
14 N ▭ rectangles* cut 2½" x 8½"
20 F ⊠ quarter-square triangles cut from 5 squares cut 7¼"
8 M ▭ rectangles* cut 3½" x 6½"
64 I ⊠ quarter-square triangles cut from 16 squares cut 5¼"
16 C ⊠ quarter-square triangles cut from 4 squares cut 4¼"
53 A ☐ squares cut 3½"
64 J ☐ squares cut 2½"
264 B ◺ half-square triangles cut from 132 squares cut 2⅜"
16 D ☐ squares cut 2"

5½ yards 44"-Wide Backing Fabric:
2 panels cut 37" x 92½"

½ yard Binding Fabric:
2" x 308"

For more stable grain, cut the K, L, M, N, and O rectangles and vertical cream strips with the long sides on the lengthwise grain of the fabric.

Read the material at the front of the book that identifies exactly what I include in my dimensions and yardage figures, tells how to get the most out of the diagrams, and details how to rotary cut and piece the Rising Star and Evening Star blocks.

Rotary cut the long cream strips first, cutting parallel to the selvage. Then cut the largest patches. They are listed in size order. Cut smaller patches from the leftovers. You need not cut everything before you start sewing. Just cut a little and sew a little.

If you wish, you can eliminate dogears by trimming the points of the B, C, E, F, H, and I triangles. Use my Point Trimmer tool or download charts and instructions for using your regular ruler to trim points by going to the RWB Extras page at

judymartin.com

For the B, E, and H triangles use the A trim of my tool or the downloaded A chart; for the C, F, and I triangles, use the B trim of my tool or the downloaded B chart.

STARS IN STRIPES BLOCKS & UNITS

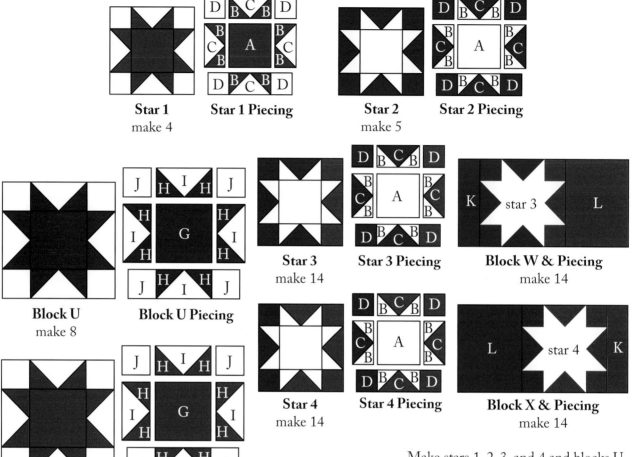

Star 1
make 4

Star 1 Piecing

Star 2
make 5

Star 2 Piecing

Block U
make 8

Block U Piecing

Star 3
make 14

Star 3 Piecing

Block W & Piecing
make 14

Block V
make 8

Block V Piecing

Star 4
make 14

Star 4 Piecing

Block X & Piecing
make 14

Make stars 1, 2, 3, and 4 and blocks U and V in the quantities listed above. Use star 1 to make block Y, star 2 to make block Z, star 3 to make block W, and star 4 to make block X, as shown.

Block Y & Piecing
make 4

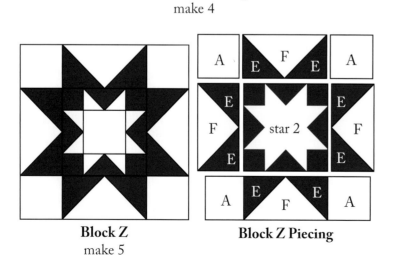

Block Z
make 5

Block Z Piecing

For this version of Stars in Stripes, substitute red for blue in diagrams and add the blue yardage and cutting list to the red.

76

STARS IN STRIPES QUILT CONSTRUCTION

Stars in Stripes Whole Quilt Construction

See the whole quilt diagram above. For the leftmost column, join 4 U and 4 V blocks and 7 N rectangles as shown. Add an O rectangle at each end to complete a pieced strip for the left side of the quilt. With the blue U star at the top, sew a 3½"-wide cream strip to the left side and a 2½"-wide strip to the right side of the pieced strip to complete the leftmost column. Repeat to make another column exactly the same for the rightmost (5th) column. The 5th column will be turned 180 degrees when it is sewn to the quilt.

For the 2nd column, join 7 X blocks alternately with 7 W blocks. Turn them so the blue ends are all on the left. This completes the 2nd column. Make the 4th column in a similar fashion, with 7 X blocks alternating with 7 W. However, this time the blue ends are all on the *right* side of the column. For the central (3rd) column, join 5 Z blocks alternately with 4 Y blocks. Add a 2"-wide strip to each side.

Lay out the 5 columns as shown above. Stitch the columns to each other to complete the quilt top.

Quilt as desired and bind to finish.

PAUL REVERE'S RIDE

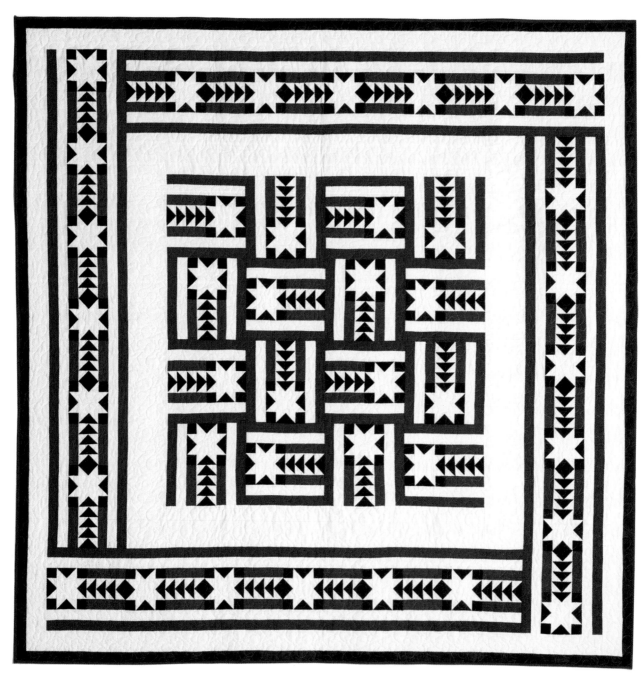

Paul Revere's Ride, 93" x 93", pieced by Mary Bird in 2020 and quilted by Vicki Bales. This quilt, with its bright stars and broad stripes, is the perfect hurrah for an American patriot, whether you are honoring Paul Revere, or a patriot in your own family.

I designed the Paul Revere's Ride block for my 2004 book, Knockout Blocks & Sampler Quilts.

Be sure to see the 2-color variation of Paul Revere's Ride on page 18.

This is an ideal quilt to make from scraps. If you do so, you can heighten the woven illlusion by piecing the 16 central blocks in 8 pairs using the same fabrics and placement in each set of two blocks and using different fabrics in other pairs. Place each horizontal pair in the same row and each vertical pair in the same column, with blocks from different pairs interspersed with them.

Be sure to note the orientation of each block and border unit as you join them to make rows.

QUILT SPECIFICATIONS

Quilt Size: 93" x 93"
Block Size: 12"
Star Size: 6"
Requires: 16 Z blocks, 40 star 1,
    40 unit 1, 40 unit 2, 4 border unit 3

YARDAGE & CUTTING

2½ yards or 10 fat quarters Red:
8 border strips* cut 2" x 72½"
32 F ▭ rectangles* cut 2" x 12½"
80 E ▭ rectangles* cut 2" x 6½"

3 yards or 12 fat quarters Navy:
2 borders* cut 2" x 93½"
2 borders* cut 2" x 90½"
320 C ⊠ quarter-square triangles cut
    from 80 squares cut 4¼"
160 D ☐ squares cut 2"

6⅛ yards Cream:
2 borders* cut 3½" x 90½"
2 borders* cut 3½" x 84½"
8 border strips* cut 2" x 72½"
2 borders* cut 6½" x 60½"
2 borders* cut 6½" x 48½"
32 F ▭ rectangles* cut 2" x 12½"
40 A ☐ squares cut 3½"
640 B ◺ half-square triangles cut from
    320 squares cut 2⅜"

9 yards 44"-Wide Backing Fabric:
3 panels cut 34¼" x 101½"

¾ yard Binding Fabric:
2" x 382"

*Cut the E and F rectangles, borders, and border strips
with the long sides on the lengthwise grain of the fabric.*

Read the material at the front of the book that identifies exactly what I include in my dimensions and yardage figures, tells how to get the most out of the diagrams, and details how to rotary cut and piece the Evening Star blocks.

Rotary cut the borders and border strips first, cutting parallel to the selvage. Then cut the largest patches. They are listed in size order. Cut smaller patches from the leftovers. You need not cut everything before you start sewing. Just cut a little and sew a little, if you like.

If you wish to trim points to eliminate dogears, see my note at the top of page 80.

Star 1
make 40

Star 1 Piecing

Unit 1
make 40

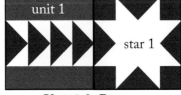

Unit 2 & Piecing
make 40

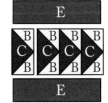

Unit 1 Piecing

Make 40 star 1's and 40 unit 1's as shown above. Use these to makes 40 unit 2's as shown.

Add cream and red F's to the top and bottom of 16 unit 2's, as shown below left, to make 16 Z blocks.

Sew 6 unit 2's in a row. Add 72½" cream and red strips to each long side, with the red on the outside edge as shown below. This completes unit 3 for the border. Repeat to make 4 border unit 3's.

Block Z & Piecing
make 16

Red and white border strips are cut 2" x 72½".

Border Unit 3
make 4

PAUL REVERE'S RIDE QUILT CONSTRUCTION

If you wish, you can eliminate dogears by trimming the points of the B and C triangles. Use my Point Trimmer tool or download charts and instructions for using your regular ruler to trim points by going to the RWB Extras page at judymartin.com For the B triangles use the A trim of my tool or A chart of your downloaded file; for the C triangles, use the B trim of my tool or the downloaded B chart.

Attach border 5 with a partial seam between green dots; complete seam after adding border 8.

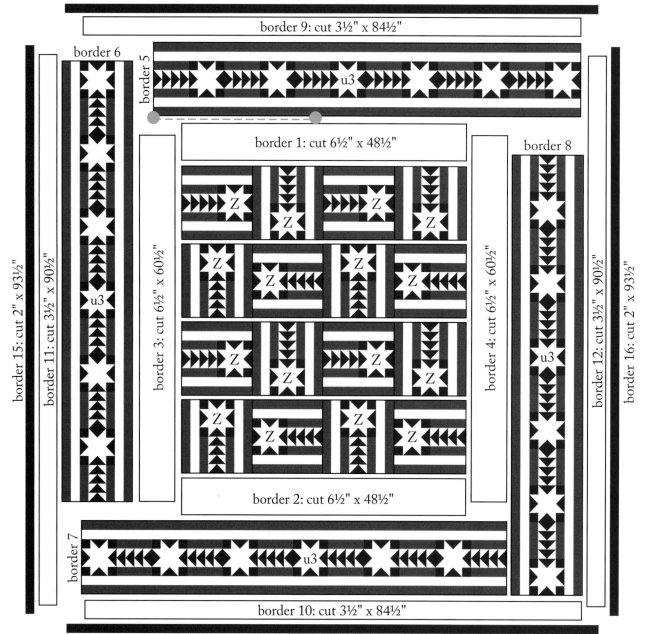

Paul Revere's Ride Whole Quilt Construction

Sew 4 Z blocks in a row, turning them as shown above. Each row is made the same; the 2nd and 4th rows are turned 180° in the quilt. Make 4 rows and join them to complete the quilt center. Add 48½" cream borders to the top and bottom. Add 60½" cream borders to the left and right.

Borders 5–8 are unit 3's. Turn them as shown. Add border 5 with a partial seam between the green dots in the quilt diagram. Add borders 6–8 in numerical order before completing the partial seam. Continue adding cream and blue borders in numerical order to complete the quilt top. Quilt and bind to finish.

80

O BEAUTIFUL!

O Beautiful!, 105" x 105", pieced by Tracey Barber of Lyons Quilting in Colorado and quilted by Donna Smith. There is nothing like a high-contrast color scheme and a big, beautiful star block to make a quilt stand out!

This block was inspired by my *Barbershop Quartet* block in The Block Book *(1998). For this 2020 quilt,* I doubled the number of small stars surrounding each big star and added the unique *Rising Star* sashing and *Evening Star* setting squares.

The quilt would be equally striking in two fabrics or in many scraps sorted into reds and creams. Be sure to see the patriotic version starting on page 85, as well.

RED/WHITE QUILT SPECIFICATIONS

for the 2-color version on pages 81–84

Quilt Size: 105" x 105"
Block Size: 27"
Star Sizes: 24", 12", 6"
Requires: 13 star 1, 36 star 2, 9 star 3, 9 X blocks, 4 Y* sashes, 8 Z* sashes

YARDAGE & CUTTING

4¾ yards or 19 fat quarters Red:
72 K ◹ half-square triangles cut from 36 squares cut 6⅞"
52 C ⊠ quarter-square triangles cut from 13 squares cut 4¼"
104 E ◹ half-square triangles cut from 52 squares cut 3⅞"
72 A ☐ squares cut 3½"
576 B ◹ half-square triangles cut from 288 squares cut 2⅜"
52 D ☐ squares cut 2"

9⅛ yards White or Cream:
2 borders** cut 6½" x 105½"
2 borders** cut 6½" x 93½"

White or Cream Yardage, *continued*

4 L ⬡ prisms* cut from 4 rectangles** cut 6½" x 27½"
8 M ⬡ half prisms* cut from 8 rectangles** cut 6½" x 27½"
36 J ☐ rectangles** cut 2" x 12½"
36 I ☐ rectangles** cut 2" x 11"
36 H ◺ half trapezoids* cut from 18 rectangles** cut 2⅝" x 7⅝"
36 Hr ◿ reversed half trapezoids* cut from 18 rectangles** cut 2⅝" x 7⅝"
36 F ⊠ quarter-square triangles cut from 9 squares cut 7¼"
180 C ⊠ quarter-square triangles cut from 45 squares cut 4¼"
49 A ☐ squares cut 3½"
36 G ☐ squares cut 2⅝"
176 B ◹ half-square triangles cut from 88 squares cut 2⅜"
144 D ☐ squares cut 2"

10 yards 44"-Wide Backing Fabric:
3 panels cut 38¼" x 113½"

¾ yard Binding Fabric:
2" x 430"

Instructions for cutting L prisms, M half prisms and H and Hr half trapezoids are shown on page 15. Hr is a reverse of H and is cut from folded fabric along with H.

**Rotary cut rectangles for H, Hr, I, J, L, and M patches and borders with the long edges on the lengthwise grain of the fabric.*

Be sure to read the material at the front of the book that explains my method, identifies exactly what I include in my dimensions and yardage figures, and teaches you how to get the most out of the diagrams.

Rotary cut the longest borders first, cutting parallel to the selvage. Then cut the shorter borders, followed by the L and M sashes. Next, proceed to the largest patches. Cut smaller patches from the leftovers. They are listed in size order, from largest to smallest.

To help you align patches for piecing, I strongly recommend trimming the points of the red B and K triangles that touch the cream G, H, and Hr patches. Use the C trim on my Point Trimmer, or download the file to make your own trimming guide from the RWB Extras page at judymartin.com

I also strongly recommend trimming the points of the 32 E triangles that will be sewn to L and M sashes. Use the A trim of my Point Trimmer tool, or download charts and instructions for using a regular rotary ruler to trim points by going to the RWB Extras page at judymartin.com

If you wish, eliminate dogears by also trimming the points of the remaining B and E triangles and all C and F triangles and H and Hr patches. Use the A trim of my Point Trimmer tool or the downloaded A chart for the B and E triangles; use the B trim of my tool or the downloaded B chart for C and F triangles; use the C trimming guide that you downloaded for B and K to trim the points of the H and Hr patches.

O BEAUTIFUL!: RED & WHITE BLOCKS & SASHES

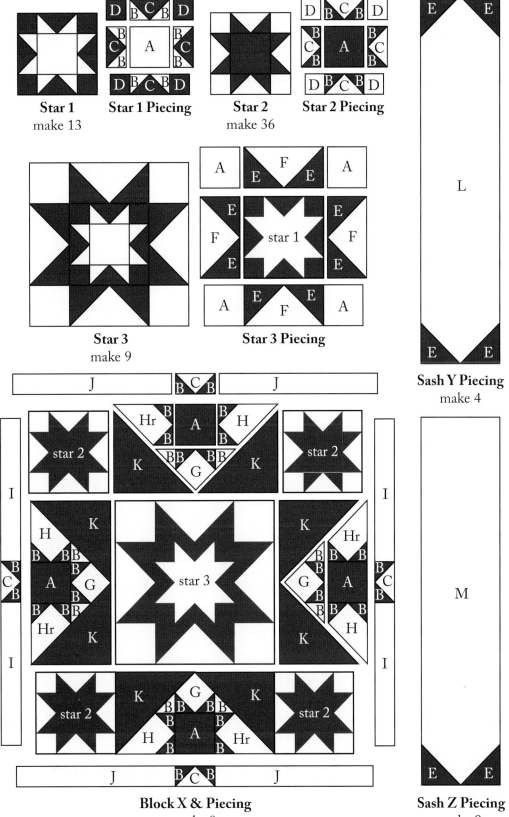

Star 1
make 13

Star 1 Piecing

Star 2
make 36

Star 2 Piecing

Star 3
make 9

Star 3 Piecing

Sash Y Piecing
make 4

Block X & Piecing
make 9

Sash Z Piecing
make 8

Referring to the figures above, make stars 1 and 2 in the listed quantities. Use 9 of the star 1's to make 9 star 3's. Reserve 4 star 1's for setting squares between sashes when you assemble the quilt.

Use stars 2 and 3 to make X blocks as shown above. The 4 stars at the center of each side are made as partial stars, with the last B-C-B added later, along with I or J rectangles.

O Beautiful! Whole Quilt Construction: Red & White

Referring to the diagrams on the previous page, make 4 Y and 8 Z sashes by adding E triangles to L and M patches.

Referring to the whole quilt construction diagram above, join X blocks, Y and Z sashes, and star 1's to make block rows and sash rows. For the top block row, join 3 X blocks alternately with 2 Z sashes, turning the Z's as shown. Repeat to make the bottom row. (It is made the same, but the row is turned 180° when you assemble the quilt.) For the center row, join 3 X blocks alternately with 2 Y sashes.

For a sash row, stitch a star 1 to each end of a Y sash; then add a Z sash to each end, turning the Z's so their red triangles touch the star 1's. Repeat to make a second sash row.

Assemble the quilt in 5 rows, alternating 3 block rows with 2 sash rows. Make sure to arrange the block rows so the ones having the Z sashes are at the top and bottom of the quilt, and the red E triangles of the sashes touch the star 1's. Add a 93½" border to the top and bottom of the quilt. Add a 105½" border to the right and left sides. Quilt and bind to finish.

RED/WHITE/BLUE QUILT SPECIFICATIONS

for the patriotic version on pages 85–87

Quilt Size: 105" x 105"
Block Size: 27"
Star Sizes: 24", 12", 6"
Requires: 13 star 1, 36 star 2, 9 star 3, 9 X blocks, 4 Y* sashes, 8 Z* sashes

YARDAGE & CUTTING

2¾ yards or 11 fat quarters Dark Blue:
72 K ◹ half-square triangles cut from 36 squares cut 6⅞"
52 C ⊠ quarter-square triangles cut from 13 squares cut 4¼"
104 E ◹ half-square triangles cut from 52 squares cut 3⅞"
52 D ☐ squares cut 2"

2⅛ yards or 9 fat quarters Red:
72 A ☐ squares cut 3½"
576 B ◹ half-square triangles cut from 288 squares cut 2⅜"

9⅛ yards White or Cream:
2 borders** cut 6½" x 105½"
2 borders** cut 6½" x 93½"

White or Cream Yardage *continued*

4 L ⬡ prisms* cut from 4 rectangles** cut 6½" x 27½"
8 M ⬡ half prisms* cut from 8 rectangles** cut 6½" x 27½"
36 J ☐ rectangles** cut 2" x 12½"
36 I ☐ rectangles** cut 2" x 11"
36 H ◺ half trapezoids* cut from 18 rectangles** cut 2⅝" x 7⅝"
36 Hr ◿ reversed half trapezoids* cut from 18 rectangles** cut 2⅝" x 7⅝"
36 F ⊠ quarter-square triangles cut from 9 squares cut 7¼"
180 C ⊠ quarter-square triangles cut from 45 squares cut 4¼"
49 A ☐ squares cut 3½"
36 G ☐ squares cut 2⅝"
176 B ◹ half-square triangles cut from 88 squares cut 2⅜"
144 D ☐ squares cut 2"

10 yards 44"-Wide Backing Fabric:
3 panels cut 38¼" x 113½"

¾ yard Binding Fabric:
2" x 430"

Instructions for cutting L prisms, M half prisms and H and Hr half trapezoids are shown on page 15. Hr is the reverse of H and is cut from folded fabric along with H.

**Rotary cut rectangles for H, Hr, I, J, L and M patches and borders with the long edges on the lengthwise grain of the fabric.*

Read the material at the front of the book that identifies exactly what I include in my dimensions and yardage figures, tells how to get the most out of the diagrams, and details how to rotary cut and piece the Rising Star and Evening Star blocks.

Rotary cut the longest borders first, cutting parallel to the selvage. Then cut the shorter borders, followed by the L and M sashes. Next, proceed to the largest patches. They are listed in size order. Cut smaller patches from the leftovers. You need not cut everything before you start sewing. After cutting the borders and sashes, you can just cut a little and sew a little before cutting more.

In order to help you align the patches for piecing, I strongly recommend trimming the points of the B and K triangles that touch the cream G, H, and Hr patches. Use the C trim on my Point Trimmer tool, or download the file to make your own point trimming guide by going to the RWB Extras page at judymartin.com

I also strongly recommend trimming the points of the 32 E triangles that will be sewn to L and M sashes. Use the A trim of my Point Trimmer tool, or download charts and instructions for using a regular rotary ruler to trim points by going to the RWB Extras page at judymartin.com

If you wish, you can eliminate dogears by also trimming the points of the remaining B and E triangles and all C and F triangles and H and Hr patches. Use the A trim of my Point Trimmer tool or the downloaded A chart for the B and E triangles; use the B trim or the downloaded B chart for C and F triangles; use the C trimming guide that you downloaded for the B and K triangles to trim points of the H and Hr patches.

O BEAUTIFUL! RED, WHITE & BLUE BLOCKS & SASHES

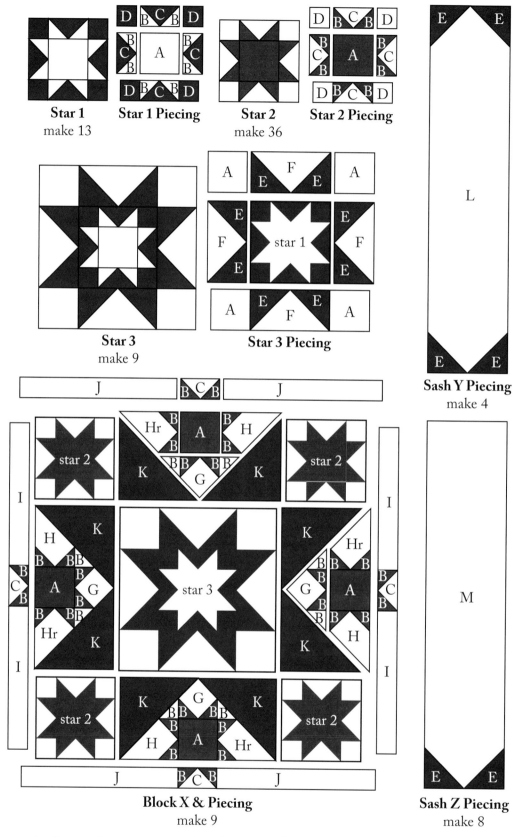

Star 1
make 13

Star 1 Piecing

Star 2
make 36

Star 2 Piecing

Sash Y Piecing
make 4

Star 3
make 9

Star 3 Piecing

Block X & Piecing
make 9

Sash Z Piecing
make 8

Referring to the figures above, make stars 1 and 2 in the listed quantities. Use 9 of the star 1's to make 9 star 3's. Reserve 4 star 1's for setting squares between sashes when you assemble the quilt.

Use stars 2 and 3 to make X blocks as shown above. The 4 stars at the center of each side are made as partial stars, with the last B-C-B added later, along with I or J rectangles.

86

border 1: cut 6½" x 93½"

border 3: cut 6½" x 105½"

border 4: cut 6½" x 105½"

border 2: cut 6½" x 93½"

O Beautiful! Whole Quilt Construction: Red, White & Blue

Referring to the diagrams on the previous page, make 4 Y and 8 Z sashes by adding blue E triangles to L and M patches.

Referring to the whole quilt construction diagram above, join X blocks, Y and Z sashes, and star 1's to make block rows and sash rows. For the top block row, join 3 X blocks alternately with 2 Z sashes, turning the Z's as shown. Repeat to make the bottom row. (It is made the same, but the row is turned 180° when you assemble the quilt.) For the center row, join 3 X blocks alternately with 2 Y sashes.

For a sash row, stitch a star 1 to each end of a Y sash; then add a Z sash to each end, turning the Z's so their dark blue triangles touch the star 1's. Repeat to make a second sash row.

Assemble the quilt in 5 rows, alternating 3 block rows with 2 sash rows. Make sure to arrange the block rows so the ones having the Z sashes are at the top and bottom of the quilt, and the blue E triangles of the sashes touch the star 1's. Add a 93½" border to the top and bottom of the quilt. Add a 105½" border to the right and left sides. Quilt and bind to finish.

AMERICA, THE BEAUTIFUL

America, the Beautiful, 76½" x 97½", pieced by me and quilted by Jean Nolte.

As a ten-year-old, my son, Will Bennett, designed this quilt on September 11, 2001. I was really proud of the way he captured the American spirit with his quilt drawing. I presented the quilt to him for Christmas. The pattern was published in my 2002 book, Piece 'n' Play Quilts. The quilt graced Will's bed at home for years. He took it with him to Chicago, where it now has a place of honor in his apartment.

QUILT SPECIFICATIONS

Quilt Size: 76½" x 97½"

Block Size: 10½" V and W, 10½" x 12" X and Y, 12" Z

Star Size: 6"

Requires: 39 star 1, 22 V, 17 W, 14 X, 10 Y, 4 Z

YARDAGE & CUTTING

2 yards or 8 fat quarters Navy Blue:

24 J ▭ rectangles* cut 3½" x 11"

156 C ⊠ quarter-square triangles cut from 39 squares cut 4¼"

156 D ▢ squares cut 2"

3⅛ yards or 13 fat quarters Red:

4 I ▭ rectangles* cut 2" x 12½"

93 H ▭ rectangles* cut 2" x 11"

39 G ▭ rectangles* cut 2" x 9½"

39 F ▭ rectangles* cut 2" x 8"

17 E ▭ rectangles* cut 2" x 6½"

4¼ yds. or 17 fat qtrs. White or Cream:

94 H ▭ rectangles* cut 2" x 11"

39 G ▭ rectangles* cut 2" x 9½"

39 F ▭ rectangles* cut 2" x 8"

22 E ▭ rectangles* cut 2" x 6½"

39 A ▢ squares cut 3½"

312 B ◺ half-square triangles cut from 156 squares cut 2⅜"

7½ yards 44"-Wide Backing Fabric:

3 panels cut 35¾" x 85"

¾ yard Binding Fabric:

2" x 358"

Rotary cut E, F, G, H, I, and J rectangles with the long edges on the lengthwise grain of the fabric.

Read the material at the front of the book that identifies exactly what I include in my dimensions and yardage figures, tells how to get the most out of the diagrams, and details how to rotary cut and piece the Evening Star blocks.

Rotary cut the patches in the order listed. They are listed in size order, starting with the largest. Cut smaller patches from the leftovers.

You need not cut everything before you start sewing, you can just cut a little and sew a little before cutting more.

If you wish, you can eliminate dogears by trimming the points of the B and C triangles. Use my Point Trimmer tool or download charts and instructions for using your regular ruler to trim points by going to the RWB Extras page at

judymartin.com

For the B triangles use the A trim of my tool or the downloaded A chart; for the C triangles, use the B trim of my tool or the downloaded B chart.

For this 2-color version of America, the Beautiful, you simply substitute cream for both navy and red, and substitute red for cream in the diagrams. You will need to add together the navy and red yardages and cutting lists to get the cream totals.

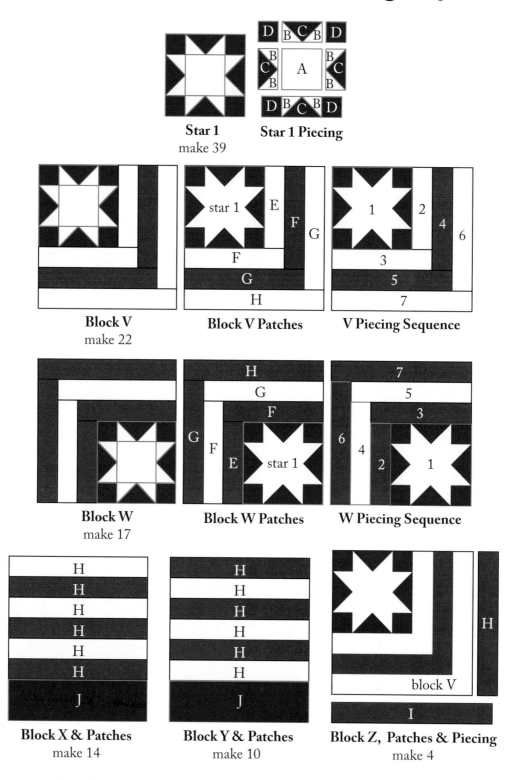

Star 1
make 39

Star 1 Piecing

Block V
make 22

Block V Patches

V Piecing Sequence

Block W
make 17

Block W Patches

W Piecing Sequence

Block X & Patches
make 14

Block Y & Patches
make 10

Block Z, Patches & Piecing
make 4

See the diagrams above. Make 39 star 1's, and use them to make blocks V and W in the quantities listed. (The quantity listed for V includes the 4 used in the Z blocks.) Refer to the patches and piecing sequence diagrams for blocks V and W as you add patches to the stars in numerical order. Press the seam allowances away from the stars when you add the rectangles.

Also make border blocks X and Y, shown above, in the quantities listed. Press the seam allowances in the X blocks toward the blue; press seam allowances away from the blue in the Y blocks.

To make the 4 Z blocks for the border corners, add a red H and a red I to each of 4 V blocks. Be sure to attach the red rectangles next to the cream ones, as shown above. Again, press seams away from the star.

AMERICA, THE BEAUTIFUL QUILT CONSTRUCTION

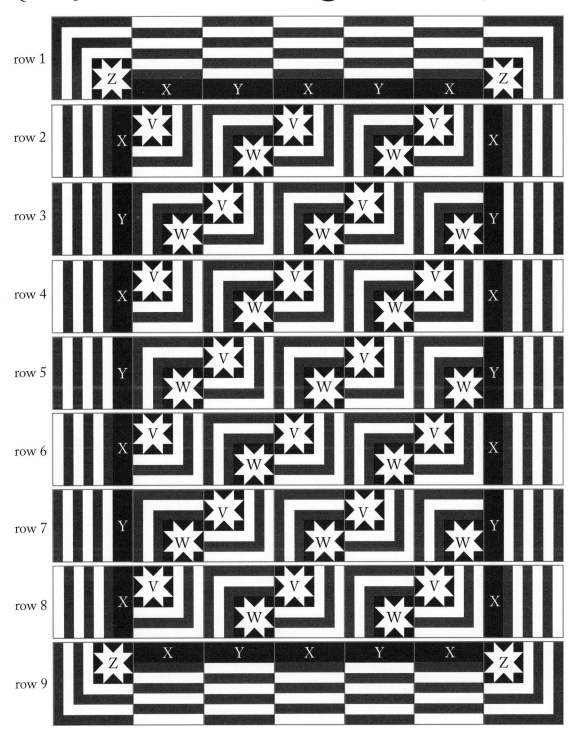

row 1
row 2
row 3
row 4
row 5
row 6
row 7
row 8
row 9

America, the Beautiful Whole Quilt Construction

Note that all V blocks are oriented with the star in the upper left corner; all W blocks have the star in the lower right corner; all Z border corners have their stripes on their outer corners; and all X and Y border blocks have the blue edge on the inside. Arrange all blocks, including border blocks, in rows as shown above.

Join blocks Z-X-Y-X-Y-X-Z in a row, keeping the blocks turned as shown above. This completes the first row. Repeat for the last row.

Join blocks X-V-W-V-W-V-X for the second row, keeping the blocks turned as shown. Repeat for rows 4, 6, and 8.

Join blocks Y-W-V-W-V-W-Y for the third row, keeping all blocks turned as shown. Repeat for rows 5 and 7.

Join the rows in the order shown to complete the quilt top. Quilt as desired and bind to finish.

MILITARY BAND

Military Band, 99" x 99", pieced by me and quilted by Debbi Treusch. I can almost hear the trumpets and the big bass drum when I see this quilt! Rising Stars and Evening Stars in two sizes and four colorings make this quilt stand out.

If you make the quilt in the patriotic colors I show here, be sure to choose a red that is a lighter value than the navy for the Rising Stars in the outer circle of the quilt center. That will make the smaller red star centers stand out against the navy stars.

My dad spent the years from 1935 to 1952 in the U.S. Navy band. He played all the brass, but most often played the trumpet or trombone. I designed this quilt in 2020, and named it in his honor.

A two-color version of Military Band in red and cream is shown on page 21.

MILITARY BAND INSTRUCTIONS

QUILT SPECIFICATIONS

Quilt Size: 99" x 99"
Block Size: 12" X and Z, 9" x 12" Y
Star Sizes: 6", 12"
Requires: 8 star 1, 12 star 2, 16 star 3, 16 star 4, 4 unit 1, 6 unit 2, 2 unit 3, 2 unit 4, 4 unit 5, 6 unit 6, 1 unit 7, 8 X blocks, 16 Y blocks, 16 Z blocks

YARDAGE & CUTTING

6½ yards or 26 fat quarters Cream:
2 borders* cut 6½" x 72½"
2 borders* cut 6½" x 60½"
2 I ▭ rectangles* cut 3½" x 18½"
1 J ▢ square cut 15½"
4 O ▢ squares cut 12½"
10 L ▭ rectangles* cut 3½" x 12½"
2 H ▭ rectangles* cut 2" x 9½"
48 F ⊠ quarter-square triangles cut from 12 squares cut 7¼"
4 K ▢ squares cut 6½"
10 G ▭ rectangles* cut 2" x 6½"
112 C ⊠ quarter-square triangles cut from 28 squares cut 4¼"
128 E ◺ half-square triangles cut from 64 squares cut 3⅞"
56 A ▢ squares cut 3½"

Cream Yardage & Cutting, *continued*
128 B ◺ half-square triangles cut from 64 squares cut 2⅜"
104 D ▢ squares cut 2"

5¼ yards or 21 fat quarters Navy:
2 borders* cut 2" x 99½"
2 borders* cut 2" x 96½"
32 N ▭ rectangles* cut 2" x 12½"
64 F ⊠ quarter-square triangles cut from 16 squares cut 7¼"
32 M ▭ rectangles* cut 3½" x 6½"
112 C ⊠ quarter-square triangles cut from 28 squares cut 4¼"
96 E ◺ half-square triangles cut from 48 squares cut 3⅞"
76 A ▢ squares cut 3½"
96 B ◺ half-square triangles cut from 48 squares cut 2⅜"
112 D ▢ squares cut 2"

1 yard or 4 or more fat quarters Red:
28 A ▢ squares cut 3½"
224 B ◺ half-square triangles cut from 112 squares cut 2⅜"

9½ yards 44"-Wide Backing Fabric:
3 panels cut 36¼" x 107½"

¾ yard Binding Fabric:
2" x 406"

Rotary cut G, H, I, L, M, and N rectangles and borders with the long edges on the lengthwise grain of the fabric.

Read the material at the front of the book that identifies exactly what I include in my dimensions and yardage figures, tells how to get the most out of the diagrams, and details how to rotary cut and piece the Rising Star and Evening Star blocks.

Cut out the patches in the dimensions and quantities listed above. Cut the borders first, then cut the largest patches. They are listed in size order. You can cut the smaller patches from the leftovers after cutting the borders and largest patches.

Though the cutting is listed first, you need not cut everything before you start sewing. In fact, I suggest that after you cut the borders and large patches, you cut a little, then sew a little before you cut the rest.

If you use scraps for the background, as I did, you can piece the borders from 44 additional K squares, with 10 squares each in left and right borders and 12 squares each in top and bottom borders.

If you wish, you can eliminate dogears by trimming the points of the B, C, E, and F triangles. Use my Point Trimmer tool or download charts and instructions for using your regular ruler to trim points by going to the RWB Extras page at
judymartin.com

For the B and E triangles, use the A trim of my tool or your downloaded file; for the C and F triangles, use the B trim of my tool or the B chart of the downloaded file.

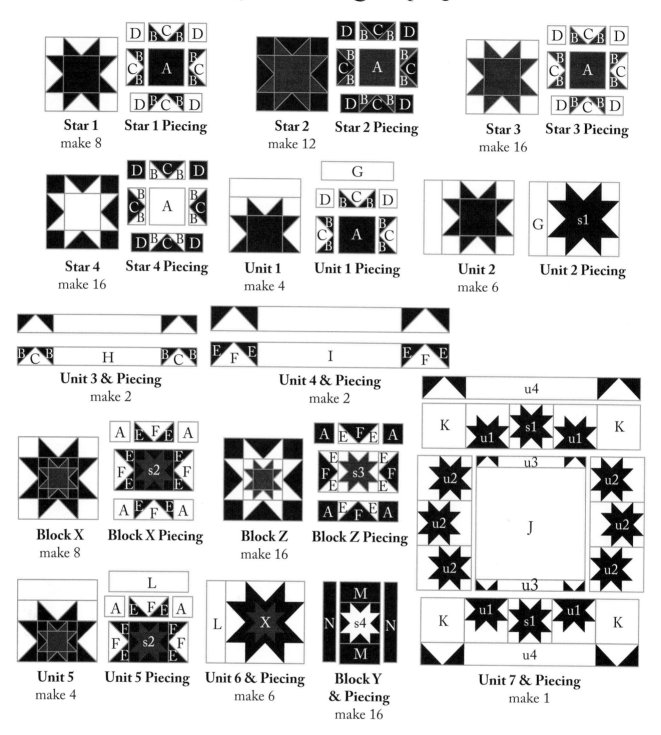

Star 1
make 8

Star 1 Piecing

Star 2
make 12

Star 2 Piecing

Star 3
make 16

Star 3 Piecing

Star 4
make 16

Star 4 Piecing

Unit 1
make 4

Unit 1 Piecing

Unit 2
make 6

Unit 2 Piecing

Unit 3 & Piecing
make 2

Unit 4 & Piecing
make 2

Block X
make 8

Block X Piecing

Block Z
make 16

Block Z Piecing

Unit 5
make 4

Unit 5 Piecing

Unit 6 & Piecing
make 6

Block Y & Piecing
make 16

Unit 7 & Piecing
make 1

Make stars 1–4, units 1–6, and blocks X, Y, and Z as shown on this page, in the listed quantities. Note that the stars in unit 1's are not completed until the rows they are in are attached to unit 7. Similarly, the stars in unit 5's are not completed until the rows they are in are sewn to unit 7, as shown on the next page.

Assemble unit 7 as follows: Sew a unit 3 to the top and bottom of the 15½" J square, with the points of the B triangles touching the J square. Join 3 unit 2's in a row, turning them so the ends having the G rectangles alternate as shown in unit 7. Repeat. Sew these rows to the right and left of the J square, as shown above. Next make a row having a star 1 flanked by 2 unit 1's, as shown above. Add a K square to each end. Repeat to make a second row. Sew one of these to the top of unit 7 and one to the bottom. Add a unit 4 to to the top and another unit 4 to the bottom, turning them as shown, to complete unit 7.

MILITARY BAND QUILT CONSTRUCTION

Military Band Whole Quilt Construction

Assemble the quilt center as shown above. The piecing echoes the piecing of unit 7, but with larger parts. Sew 3 unit 6's in a row, turning them so the ends having the L rectangles alternate as shown in the whole quilt diagram. Repeat. Sew these rows to the right and left of the unit 7, as shown above. Next make a row having an X block flanked by 2 unit 5's, as shown above. Add a 12½" O square to each end. Repeat to make a second row. Sew one of these rows to the top of the quilt center and one to the bottom. Add a 6½ x 60½" border to the right and left sides.

Make the top pieced border by alternating 4 Y blocks with 3 Z blocks in a row. Attach a 6½" x 72½" border. Attach to the top of the quilt with the plain border on the inside. Repeat for the bottom.

Make a side pieced border by alternating 5 Z blocks with 4 Y blocks. Add a 2" x 96½" border. Attach to the left side of the quilt, with the blue border on the outside edge. Repeat for the right side of the quilt.

Add a 2" x 99½" blue border to the top of the quilt. Repeat for the bottom to complete the top.

JUDY MARTIN BOOKS

Singular Stars, 2018, 160 pages. 17 photographed quilts and 59 accurate strip-piecing patterns for fresh, new Lone Stars plus 124 surprisingly different variations you can make from the same patterns. Plenty of queen- to king-sized masterpieces as well as simple, little Lone Stars. Expert tips and detailed how-to's. Nearly 1000 color illustrations. "You really have taken Lone Stars to a whole new level. *Singular Stars* goes above and beyond any other quilt book..."
– Linda Franz, author, quilter

Extraordinary Log Cabin Quilts, 2013, 128 pages. 15 fresh, new patterns presented in multiple sizes, each with 12 or more setting or coloring variations. Expert tips on everything from choosing values to rotary cutting and sewing. "These designs just blow my mind!" – Bonnie K. Hunter, author, quilter

Patchwork Among Friends, 2011, 128 pages. 10 glorious patterns, 12 tasty potluck supper recipes. Each pattern is presented in two sizes, complete with color diagrams, pressing instructions, and cutting layouts. Find great ideas for quilt get-togethers. "Go order a copy of *Patchwork Among Friends* - it's really, really good! Gorgeous quilt patterns!" – Tara Darr, Sew Unique Creations, Joliet, IL

Stellar Quilts, 2010, 128 pages. 13 patterns for outstanding star quilts in multiple sizes. Includes additional colorings for each. "Your quilts are fabulous. *Stellar Quilts* took my breath away." – Mary V., Lincoln, NE "Judy designs quilts like no other....complex looking, but not necessarily complex in construction." – *American Quilt Retailer*

Judy Martin's Log Cabin Quilt Book, 2007, 128 pages. 16 Log Cabins and exciting variations are presented in multiple sizes. This lavishly illustrated book has 150 color photos, 100 setting plans, 45 log borders, charts, and more. "As usual, Judy's instructions are precise, complete and easy to follow." – Helen Weinman, Heartbeat Quilts, Hyannis, MA

Piece 'n' Play Quilts, 2002, 96 pages. Complete patterns for 12 new and easy Drunkard's Paths, Log Cabins, and more. First you follow the pattern and piece the blocks. Then you play with their arrangement until you find the look YOU want. "*Piece 'n' Play Quilts* is a great book for beginners as well as the more experienced quilter." – Patricia T., Pahoa, HI

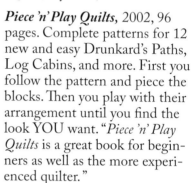

Cookies 'n' Quilts, 2001, 80 pages. 8 original quilt patterns feature interesting combinations such as stars within stars or Snail's Trails made entirely from logs. The cookies and bars will take your baking to a new level of delicious decadence. "The book is well worth every penny, even if you buy it for the quilt patterns alone." – Sophie Littlefield, QuiltersReview.com

Judy Martin's Ultimate Rotary Cutting Reference, 1997, 80 pages. You'll find charts and instructions for cutting 52 shapes in countless sizes, plus yardage figures and information on tools and techniques. "*Judy Martin's Ultimate Rotary Cutting Reference* will show you how to make the most of the rotary cutting rulers and tools you already own to cut shapes you didn't think were possible to rotary cut."
– Liz Porter, "Love of Quilting"

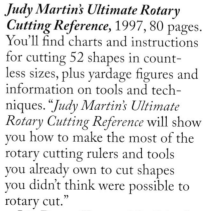

for more information about these products plus instructional videos, reader photos, and more visit
judymartin.com